Promises
from GOD

B O O K   T W O

Promises from GOD

from GOD

BOOK TWO

COMPILED BY
SAMUEL CLARKE, D.D.

SPIRE

Reprinted in 2003 by Fleming H. Revell
a division of Baker Book House Company
P.O. Box 6287, Grand Rapids, MI 49516–6287
www.bakerbooks.com

Formerly published as part of *Precious Bible Promises* by Fleming H.
Revell in 1971.

Printed in the United States of America

ISBN 0-8007-8709-9

Scripture is taken from the King James Version of the Bible.

Notice by Dr. Watts

The Bible is a book of such transcendent worth, and so happily suited to all the parts and purposes of the Christian life, that it can never be too much recommended to the world; every thing that allures the world to peruse it, is a blessing to mankind. And though it is hard for our narrow capacities to grasp and take in its several distinguishing excellences at one view, yet, if we take a separate survey of the doctrines and duties, the promises and threatenings, the prophecies and histories, which are contained therein, each of them will afford us an awful or a delightful prospect, with lessons for special improvement.

The worthy author of this collection, which I have long known with esteem and honor, has chosen to reduce all the most useful and important promises of the Word of God into order, and here set them before us. These are the most powerful motives of duty; these are the constant food of a living Christian, as well as his highest cordials in a fainting hour. And in such a world as this, where duties perpetually demand our practice, and difficulties and trials are ever surrounding us, what can we do better than to treasure up the promises in our hearts, which are the most effectual persuasives to fulfil the one and sustain the other? Here are laid up the true riches of a Christian, and his highest hopes on this side of heaven.

The materials which are collected here are all divine, and the disposition of them is elegant and regular; so that it is an easy matter to find something suited to the frame of our souls, or our present wants on every occasion; and that soul who knows what a suitable promise is worth in an hour of darkness or temptation, will never think such a work as this, and such a various treasure, can have sufficient value set upon it.

Those who have little leisure for reading, may find their account in keeping this book always near them; and with the glance of an eye they may take in the riches of grace and glory, and derive many a sweet refreshment from hence, amidst their labors and travels through this wilderness. It is of excellent use to lie on the table in a chamber of sickness, and now and then to take a sip of the river of life, which runs through it in a thousand little rills of peace and joy.

May the Holy Spirit of God, who indited all these promises, and our blessed Mediator, who, by his ministry and by his blood, has sealed and confirmed them all, render them every day more and more powerful and prevalent to draw the hearts of men towards God, and to fit them for the enjoyment of these words of grace in the complete accomplishment in glory. Amen.

I. WATTS
NEWINGTON, JANUARY 19, 1750

Contents

❦

Promises for the Exercise of Duties
and Glories

Promises of the Growth and Glory of the Church

Promises of Christ's Second Coming

Conclusion

Helpful Thoughts for Special Occasions

Promises for the Exercise of Duties and Glories

One

In the Fulfillment of Duty toward God

1. TO FAITH IN CHRIST

Behold, I lay in Zion for a foundation a stone, a tried stone, a precious corner stone, a sure foundation. He that believeth, shall not make haste.　　ISAIAH 28:16

He that believeth on him shall not be confounded.
　　1 PETER 2:6

I am come a light into the world, that whosoever believeth on me should not abide in darkness.
　　JOHN 12:46

God so loved the world, that he gave his only begotten Son, that whosoever believeth in him should not perish, but have everlasting life. He that believeth on him is not condemned. He that believeth on the Son hath everlasting life.　　JOHN 3:16, 18, 36; 6:47

By grace are ye saved, through faith. EPHESIANS 2:8

Thy faith hath saved thee; go in peace. LUKE 7:50

Look unto me, and be ye saved, all the ends of the earth. ISAIAH 45:22

If thou canst believe, all things are possible to him that believeth. MARK 9:23

Christ is the end of the law for righteousness to every one that believeth. ROMANS 10:4

Believe on the Lord Jesus Christ, and thou shalt be saved, and thy house. ACTS 16:31

Behold, I lay in Zion a stumblingstone, and rock of offence; and whosoever believeth on him shall not be ashamed. ROMANS 9:33

To him that worketh not, but believeth on Him that justifieth the ungodly, his faith is counted for righteousness. ROMANS 4:5

To him give all the prophets witness, that, through his name, whosoever believeth in him shall receive remission of sins. ACTS 10:43

Come unto me, all ye that labor and are heavy laden, and I will give you rest. MATTHEW 11:28

The just shall live by faith. We are of them that believe, to the saving of the soul. HEBREWS 10:38–39

And Jesus said unto them, I am the bread of life; he that cometh to me shall never hunger, and he that believeth on me shall never thirst. All that the Father giveth me, shall come to me; and him that cometh to me I will in no wise cast out.   JOHN 6:35, 37

They which be of faith are blessed with faithful Abraham. They which are of faith, the same are the children of Abraham. The scripture hath concluded all under sin, that the promise by faith of Jesus Christ might be given to them that believe.   GALATIANS 3:9, 7, 22

To whom coming, as unto a living stone, disallowed indeed of men, but chosen of God, and precious, ye also, as lively stones, are built up a spiritual house, a holy priesthood, to offer up spiritual sacrifices, acceptable to God by Jesus Christ.   1 PETER 2:4–5

Blessed are they that have not seen, and yet have believed.   JOHN 20:29

We trust in the living God, who is the Saviour of all men, especially of those that believe. 1 TIMOTHY 4:10

That ye be not slothful, but followers of them who through faith and patience inherit the promises.
                                        HEBREWS 6:12

As many as received him, to them gave he power to become the sons of God, even to them that believe on his name.   JOHN 1:12

Confessing Christ

Whosoever shall confess that Jesus is the Son of God, God dwelleth in him, and he in God.   1 JOHN 4:15

Whosoever shall confess me before men, him will I confess also before my Father which is in heaven.

MATTHEW 10:32

If thou shalt confess with thy mouth the Lord JESUS, and shalt believe in thy heart that God hath raised him from the dead, thou shalt be saved. For with the heart man believeth unto righteousness; and with the mouth confession is made unto salvation.   ROMANS 10:9–10

2. TO REPENTANCE

That they may return every man from his evil way, that I may forgive their iniquity and their sin.

JEREMIAH 36:3

Turn ye unto me, saith the LORD of hosts, and I will turn unto you, saith the LORD of hosts.

ZECHARIAH 1:3; MALACHI 3:7

The LORD your God is gracious and merciful, and will not turn away his face from you, if ye return unto him.   2 CHRONICLES 30:9

O Jerusalem, wash thy heart from wickedness, that thou mayest be saved. How long shall thy vain thoughts lodge within thee?   JEREMIAH 4:14

If my people, which are called by my name, shall humble themselves, and pray, and seek my face, and turn from their wicked ways; then will I hear and will forgive their sin. 2 CHRONICLES 7:14

If so be they will hearken, and turn every man from his evil way, that I may repent me of the evil which I purpose to do unto them, because of the evil of their doings. Amend your ways and your doings, and obey the voice of the LORD your God; and the LORD will repent him of the evil that he hath pronounced against you. JEREMIAH 26:3, 13

If that nation, against whom I have pronounced, turn from their evil, I will repent of the evil that I thought to do unto them. JEREMIAH 18:8

Let the wicked forsake his way, and the unrighteous man his thoughts, and let him return unto the LORD, and he will have mercy upon him; and to our God, for he will abundantly pardon. ISAIAH 55:7

If the wicked will turn from all his sins that he hath committed, and keep all my statutes, and do that which is lawful and right, he shall surely live, he shall not die. All his transgressions that he hath committed, they shall not be mentioned unto him: in his righteousness that he hath done, he shall live. Have I any pleasure at all that the wicked should die, saith the Lord GOD, and not that he should return from his ways and live? Repent, and turn yourselves from all your transgressions; so iniquity shall not be your ruin. Cast away from you all your transgressions whereby ye have transgressed, and make you a new heart, and a new spirit: for why will ye die, O house of Israel? For I have no pleasure in the death of him that dieth, saith the Lord GOD: wherefore turn yourselves, and live ye.   EZEKIEL 18:21–23, 30–32

Depart from evil and do good, and dwell for evermore.
PSALM 37:27

Turn you at my reproof: behold, I will pour out my spirit unto you, I will make known my words unto you.
PROVERBS 1:23

Turn ye even to me with all your heart, and with fasting, and with weeping, and with mourning; and rend your heart and not your garments, and turn unto the LORD your God; for he is gracious and merciful, slow to anger, and of great kindness, and repenteth him of the evil. Who knoweth if he will return and repent, and leave a blessing behind him, even a meat-offering and a drink-offering unto the LORD your God?   JOEL 2:12–14

When I say unto the wicked, Thou shalt surely die; if he turn from his sin, and do that which is lawful and right; if the wicked restore the pledge, give again that he had robbed, walk in the statutes of life, without committing iniquity, he shall surely live, he shall not die. None of his sins that he hath committed shall be mentioned unto him; he hath done that which is lawful and right. If the wicked turn from his wickedness, and do that which is lawful and right, he shall live thereby.
EZEKIEL 33:14–16, 19

If thou return to the Almighty, thou shalt be built up, thou shalt put away iniquity far from thy tabernacles.
JOB 22:23

Awake, thou that sleepest, and arise from the dead, and Christ shall give thee light.　EPHESIANS 5:14

Repent, and be baptized, every one of you, in the name of Jesus Christ, for the remission of sins, and ye shall receive the gift of the Holy Ghost.　ACTS 2:38

Repent ye, therefore, and be converted, that your sins may be blotted out, when the times of refreshing shall come from the presence of the Lord.　ACTS 3:19

To Them That Mourn for the Wickedness of the Land

Go through the midst of the city, and set a mark upon the foreheads of the men that sigh and that cry for all the abominations that be done in the midst thereof. Slay utterly old and young; but come not near any man upon whom is the mark.　EZEKIEL 9:4, 6

Repenting in Affliction

Come, and let us return unto the LORD; for he hath torn, and he will heal us: he hath smitten, and he will bind us up.　HOSEA 6:1

He looketh upon men; and if any say, I have sinned and perverted that which was right, and it profited me not; he will deliver his soul from going into the pit, and his life shall see the light.   JOB 33:27–28

When thou art in tribulation, and all these things are come upon thee, even in the latter days, if thou turn to the LORD thy God, and shalt be obedient to his voice; (for the LORD thy God is a merciful God); he will not forsake thee, neither destroy thee, nor forget the covenant of thy fathers, which he sware unto them.
                                    DEUTERONOMY 4:30–31

If thou shalt return unto the LORD thy God, and shalt obey his voice, according to all that I command thee this day, thou and thy children, with all thy heart, and with all thy soul; then the LORD thy God will turn thy captivity, and have compassion upon thee, and will return and gather thee from all the nations whither the LORD thy God hath scattered thee. And thou shalt return, and obey the voice of the LORD, and do all his commandments, which I command thee this day.   DEUTERONOMY 30:2–3, 8

Confession of Sin

Whoso confesseth and forsaketh them, shall have mercy.   PROVERBS 28:13

I said, I will confess my transgressions unto the LORD; and thou forgavest the iniquity of my sin. Thou art my hiding place; thou shalt preserve me.   PSALM 32:5, 7

If we confess our sins, he is faithful and just to forgive us our sins, and to cleanse us from all unrighteousness.
                                    1 JOHN 1:9

The son said unto him, Father, I have sinned against heaven, and in thy sight, and am no more worthy to be called thy son. But the father said to his servants, Bring forth the best robe, and put it on him, and put a ring on his hand, and shoes on his feet.   LUKE 15:21–22

If they shall confess their iniquity, and the iniquity of their fathers, with their trespass which they trespassed against me, and that also they have walked contrary unto me; and that I also have walked contrary unto them, and have brought them into the land of their enemies: if then their uncircumcised hearts be humbled, and they then accept of the punishment of their iniquity: then will I remember my covenant with Jacob, and also my covenant with Isaac, and also my covenant with Abraham will I remember; and I will remember the land.
LEVITICUS 26:40–42

Return, thou backsliding Israel, saith the LORD, and I will not cause mine anger to fall upon you: for I am merciful, saith the LORD, and I will not keep anger for ever. Only acknowledge thine iniquity, that thou hast transgressed against the LORD thy God, and hast scattered thy ways to the strangers under every green tree, and ye have not obeyed my voice, saith the LORD.
JEREMIAH 3:12–13

3. OBEDIENCE

Blessed are they that keep judgment, and he that doeth righteousness, at all times.   PSALM 106:3

Whosoever shall do and teach these commandments, the same shall be called great in the kingdom of heaven.

MATTHEW 5:19

Hearken, O Israel, unto the statutes, and unto the judgments which I teach you, for to do them, that ye may live, and go in and possess the land which the Lord God of your fathers giveth you. Keep therefore and do them, for this is your wisdom, and your understanding in the sight of the nations, which shall hear all these statutes, and say, Surely this great nation is a wise and understanding people.

DEUTERONOMY 4:1, 6

Keep therefore the words of this covenant, and do them, that ye may prosper in all that ye do.

DEUTERONOMY 29:9

A blessing, if ye obey the commandments of the LORD your God, which I command you this day.

DEUTERONOMY 11:27

O that there were such a heart in them, that they would fear me, and keep all my commandments always that it might be well with them, and with their children for ever.

DEUTERONOMY 5:29

It shall come to pass, if ye hearken to these judgments, and keep and do them, that the LORD thy God shall keep unto thee the covenant and the mercy which he sware unto thy fathers.

DEUTERONOMY 7:12

Hear, therefore, O Israel, and observe to do it; that it may be well with thee, and that ye may increase mightily, as the LORD God of thy fathers hath promised thee, in the land that floweth with milk and honey. Thou shalt do that which is right and good in the sight of the LORD, that it may be well with thee, and that thou mayest go in and possess the good land, which the LORD sware unto thy fathers, to cast out all thine enemies from before thee, as the LORD hath spoken.

DEUTERONOMY 6:3, 18–19

Ye shall do my statutes, and keep my judgments, and do them; and ye shall dwell in the land in safety. And the land shall yield her fruit; and ye shall eat your fill, and dwell therein in safety.   LEVITICUS 25:18–19

If ye will fear the LORD and serve him, and obey his voice, and not rebel against the commandment of the LORD; then shall both ye, and also the king that reigneth over you, continue following the LORD your God.

1 SAMUEL 12:14

Set your hearts unto all the words which I testify among you this day; which ye shall command your children to observe to do all the words of this law. For it is not a vain thing for you, because it is your life; and through this thing ye shall prolong your days in the land whither ye go over Jordan to possess it.

DEUTERONOMY 32:46–47

That the LORD may turn from the fierceness of his anger, and show thee mercy, and have compassion upon thee, and multiply thee, as he hath sworn unto thy fathers; when thou shalt hearken to the voice of the LORD thy God, to keep all his commandments which I command thee this day, to do that which is right in the eyes of the LORD thy God. DEUTERONOMY 13:17–18

Be ye strong therefore, and let not your hand be weak, for your work shall be rewarded. 2 CHRONICLES 15:7

All the paths of the LORD are mercy and truth unto such as keep his covenant and his testimonies.

PSALM 25:10

If they obey and serve him, they shall spend their days in prosperity, and their years in pleasures.

JOB 36:11

If ye will obey my voice indeed, and keep my covenant, then ye shall be a peculiar treasure unto me above all people. EXODUS 19:5

Blessed are the undefiled in the way, who walk in the law of the LORD. Blessed are they that keep his testimonies, and that seek him with the whole heart. Then shall I not be ashamed, when I have respect unto all thy commandments. PSALM 119:1–2, 6

The LORD give thee wisdom and understanding, and give thee charge concerning Israel, that thou mayest keep the law of the LORD thy God; then shalt thou prosper, if thou takest heed to fulfil the statutes and judgments which the LORD charged Moses with concerning Israel. 1 CHRONICLES 22:12–13

He that keepeth the commandment, keepeth his own soul. PROVERBS 19:16

O that thou hadst hearkened to my commandments! Then had thy peace been as a river, and thy righteousness as the waves of the sea.   ISAIAH 48:18

Blessed are they that do his commandments, that they may have right to the tree of life, and may enter in through the gates into the city.   REVELATION 22:14

Obey my voice, and I will be your God, and ye shall be my people; and walk ye in all the ways that I have commanded you, that it may be well unto you.
                                                    JEREMIAH 7:23

Keep the charge of the LORD thy God, to walk in his ways, to keep his statutes, and his commandments, and his judgments, and his testimonies, that thou mayest prosper in all that thou doest, and whithersoever thou turnest thyself.   1 KINGS 2:3

See, I have set before thee this day life and good, and death and evil: in that I command thee this day to love the LORD thy God, to walk in his ways, and keep his commandments, and his statutes, and his judgments, that thou mayest live and multiply; and the LORD thy God shall bless thee.   DEUTERONOMY 30:15–16

He that doeth the will of God abideth for ever.
                                                    1 JOHN 2:17

If ye know these things, happy are ye if ye do them.
                                                    JOHN 13:17

PROMISES FOR THE EXCERCISE OF DUTIES AND GLORIES

To him that ordereth his conversation aright, will I show the salvation of God.   PSALM 50:23

If any man will do his will, he shall know of the doctrine whether it be of God, or whether I speak of myself.
JOHN 7:17

Whosoever shall do the will of my Father which is in heaven, the same is my brother, and sister, and mother.
MATTHEW 12:50

Whatsoever we ask, we receive of him, because we keep his commandments, and do those things that are pleasing in his sight.   1 JOHN 3:22

Not every one that saith unto me, Lord, Lord, shall enter into the kingdom of heaven; but he that doeth the will of my Father which is in heaven. MATTHEW 7:21

Whoso looketh into the perfect law of liberty, and continueth therein, he being not a forgetful hearer, but a doer of the work, this man shall be blessed in his deed.
JAMES 1:25

He that keepeth the law, happy is he.
PROVERBS 29:18

The doers of the law shall be justified. ROMANS 2:13

If ye be willing and obedient, ye shall eat the good of the land.   ISAIAH 1:19

Those things which ye have both learned, and received, and heard, and seen in me, do; and the God of peace shall be with you. PHILIPPIANS 4:9

Obeying Christ

If ye keep my commandments, ye shall abide in my love. JOHN 15:10

He became the author of eternal salvation unto all them that obey him. HEBREWS 5:9

If thou shalt indeed obey his [the angel's] voice, and do all that I speak; then I will be an enemy unto thine enemies, and an adversary unto thine adversaries. EXODUS 29:22

Who is among you that feareth the LORD, that obeyeth the voice of his servant, that walketh in darkness, and hath no light? Let him trust in the name of the LORD, and stay upon his God. ISAIAH 50:10

If a man keep my saying, he shall never see death. JOHN 8:51

He that heareth my word, and believeth on him that sent me, hath everlasting life, and shall not come into condemnation, but is passed from death unto life. JOHN 5:24

Whosoever heareth these sayings of mine, and doeth them, I will liken him unto a wise man which built his house upon a rock; and the rain descended, and the floods came, and the winds blew, and beat upon that house, and it fell not; for it was founded upon a rock.

MATTHEW 7:24–25

4. TO SINCERITY AND UPRIGHTNESS

With an upright man thou wilt show thyself upright.

PSALM 18:25

I know also, my God, that thou hast pleasure in uprightness.   1 CHRONICLES 29:17

The righteous LORD loveth righteousness: his countenance doth behold the upright.   PSALM 11:7

The eyes of the LORD run to and fro throughout the whole earth, to show himself strong in behalf of them whose heart is perfect towards him.   2 CHRONICLES 16:9

The way of the LORD is strength to the upright.

PROVERBS 10:29

Righteousness keepeth him that is upright in the way.

PROVERBS 13:6

Let my heart be sound in thy statutes, that I be not ashamed.   PSALM 119:80

Do good, O LORD, unto those that be good, and to them that are upright in their hearts.   PSALM 125:4

The LORD knoweth the days of the upright; and their inheritance shall be for ever.   PSALM 37:18

LORD, who shall abide in thy tabernacle? Who shall dwell in thy holy hill? He that walketh uprightly, and worketh righteousness.   PSALM 15:1–2

The integrity of the upright shall guide them. The righteousness of the upright shall deliver them. Such as are upright in their way are his delight.

PROVERBS 11:3, 6, 20

He layeth up sound wisdom for the righteous; he is a buckler to them that walk uprightly. The upright shall dwell in the land, and the perfect shall remain in it.

PROVERBS 2:7, 21

The prayer of the upright is his delight.

PROVERBS 15:8

They that deal truly are his delight. PROVERBS 12:22

Do not my words do good to him that walketh uprightly?   MICAH 1:7

If our heart condemn us not, then have we confidence towards God.   1 JOHN 3:21

Happy is he that condemneth not himself in that thing which he alloweth.   ROMANS 14:22

The wicked shall be a ransom for the righteous, and the transgressor for the upright.   PROVERBS 21:18

If thou wert pure and upright, surely now he would awake for thee, and make the habitation of thy righteousness prosperous. JOB 8:6

Whoso causeth the righteous to go astray in an evil way, he shall fall himself into his own pit; but the upright shall have good things in possession. Whoso walketh uprightly shall be saved. A faithful man shall abound with blessings. PROVERBS 28:10, 18, 20

5. TO THE LOVE OF GOD

God, that keepeth covenant and mercy for them that love him. NEHEMIAH 1:5

All things work together for good to them that love God. ROMANS 8:28

Because he hath set his love upon me, therefore will I deliver him. PSALM 91:14

Delight thyself also in the LORD, and he shall give thee the desires of thy heart. PSALM 37:4

Showing mercy unto thousands of them that love me, and keep my commandments. EXODUS 20:6

God, which keepeth covenant and mercy with them that love him and keep his commandments, to a thousand generations. DEUTERONOMY 7:9

It shall come to pass, if ye shall hearken diligently unto my commandments, which I command you this day, to love the LORD your God, and to serve him with all your heart, and with all your soul; that I will give you the rain of your land in his due season, the first rain, and the latter rain, that thou mayest gather in thy corn, and thy wine, and thine oil.   DEUTERONOMY 11:13–14

The LORD preserveth all them that love him.
                                    PSALM 145:20

If any man love God, the same is known of him.
                                    1 CORINTHIANS 8:3

Let them that love him be as the sun, when he goeth forth in his might.   JUDGES 5:31

Heirs of the kingdom, which he hath promised to them that love him.   JAMES 2:5

Eye hath not seen, nor ear heard, neither have entered into the heart of man, the things which God hath prepared for them that love him.   1 CORINTHIANS 2:9

O Lord, the great and dreadful God, keeping the covenant and mercy to them that love him, and to them that keep his commandments.   DANIEL 9:4

To the Love of Christ

He that loveth me, shall be loved of my Father; and I will love him, and will manifest myself to him.
                                    JOHN 14:21

A crown of righteousness, which the Lord, the righteous Judge, shall give me at that day; and not to me only, but unto all them also that love his appearing.

2 TIMOTHY 4:8

Grace be with all of them that love our Lord Jesus Christ in sincerity. EPHESIANS 6:24

The crown of life, which the Lord hath promised to them that love him. JAMES 1:12

I love them that love me. That I may cause those that love me to inherit substance, and I will fill their treasures.

PROVERBS 8:17, 21

6. TO TRUSTING AND WAITING PATIENTLY ON GOD

He is a buckler to all those that trust in him.

PSALM 18:30

Blessed are all they that put their trust in him.

PSALM 2:12

They that trust in the LORD shall be as mount Zion, which cannot be removed, but abideth for ever.

PSALM 125:1

Wait on the LORD; be of good courage, and he shall strengthen thy heart; wait, I say, on the LORD.

PSALM 27:14

Oh how great is thy goodness, which thou hast laid up for them that fear thee; which thou hast wrought for them that trust in thee before the sons of men! Be of good courage, and he shall strengthen your heart, all ye that hope in the LORD.   PSALM 31:19, 24

I have trusted in the LORD, therefore I shall not slide.
                                                      PSALM 26:1

The LORD is good: blessed is the man that trusteth in him.   PSALM 34:8; 84:12

Blessed is the man that maketh the LORD his trust, and respecteth not the proud, nor such as turn aside to lies.
                                                      PSALM 40:4

In God I will praise his word, in God I have put my trust; I will not fear what flesh can do unto me.
                                                      PSALM 56:4

Lo, this is our God; we have waited for him, and he will save us: this is the LORD; we have waited for him, we will be glad and rejoice in his salvation.
                                                      ISAIAH 25:9

He shall not be afraid of evil tidings: his heart is fixed, trusting in the LORD. His heart is established, he shall not be afraid, until he see his desire upon his enemies.
                                                      PSALM 112:7–8

Trust in the LORD, and do good; so shalt thou dwell in the land, and verily thou shalt be fed. Those that wait upon the LORD, they shall inherit the earth. The LORD shall help them, and deliver them: he shall deliver them from the wicked, and save them, because they trust in him.   PSALM 37:3, 9, 40

Blessed are all they that wait for him.   ISAIAH 30:18

They shall not be ashamed that wait for me.
                                                                ISAIAH 49:23

He that putteth his trust in the LORD shall be made fat.
                                                                PROVERBS 28:25

Happy is he that hath the God of Jacob for his help, whose hope is in the LORD his God.   PSALM 146:5

Commit thy works unto the LORD, and thy thoughts shall be established. Whoso trusteth in the LORD, happy is he.   PROVERBS 16:3, 20

Thou wilt keep him in perfect peace, whose mind is stayed on thee; because he trusteth in thee. Trust ye in the LORD for ever; for in the LORD Jehovah is everlasting strength.   ISAIAH 26:3–4

Blessed is the man that trusteth in the LORD, and whose hope the LORD is. For he shall be as a tree planted by the waters, and that spreadeth out her roots by the river, and shall not see when heat cometh, but her leaves shall be green; and shall not be careful in the year of drought, neither shall cease from yielding fruit.
                                                              JEREMIAH 17:7–8

We are saved by hope.   ROMANS 8:24

He knoweth them that trust in him.   NAHUM 1:7

Whoso putteth his trust in the LORD shall be safe.
PROVERBS 29:25

Casting all your care upon him, for he careth for you.
1 PETER 5:7

I will look unto the LORD, I will wait for the God of my salvation; my God will hear me.   MICAH 7:7

He that putteth his trust in me shall possess the land and shall inherit my holy mountain.   ISAIAH 57:13

The LORD redeemeth the soul of his servants, and none of them that trust in him shall be desolate.
PSALM 34:22

The LORD is good unto them that wait for him, to the soul that seeketh him. It is good that a man should both hope, and quietly wait for the salvation of the LORD.
LAMENTATIONS 3:25–26

7. TO THE FEAR OF GOD

Surely his salvation is nigh them that fear him.
PSALM 85:9

He will bless them that fear the LORD, both small and great.   PSALM 115:13

By the fear of the LORD men depart from evil.
PROVERBS 16:6

It shall be well with them that fear God, which fear before him. ECCLESIASTES 8:12

Blessed is every one that feareth the LORD, that walketh in his ways. PSALM 128:1

O how great is thy goodness, which thou hast laid up for them that fear thee. PSALM 31:19

The secret of the LORD is with them that fear him, and he will show them his covenant. PSALM 25:14

As the heaven is high above the earth, so great is his mercy toward them that fear him. PSALM 103:11

Be not wise in thine own eyes: fear the LORD, and depart from evil. It shall be health to thy navel, and marrow to thy bones. PROVERBS 3:7–8

In the fear of the LORD is strong confidence, and his children shall have a place of refuge. The fear of the LORD is a fountain of life, to depart from the snares of death. PROVERBS 14:26–27

The LORD taketh pleasure in them that fear him. PSALM 147:11

His mercy is on them that fear him, from generation to generation. LUKE 1:50

Whosoever among you feareth God, to you is the word of this salvation sent. ACTS 13:26

In every nation he that feareth him, and worketh righteousness, is accepted with him.   Acts 10:35

Unto you that fear my name shall the Sun of righteousness arise with healing in his wings. Malachi 4:2

The fear of the Lord tendeth to life, and he that hath it shall abide satisfied: he shall not be visited with evil.
          Proverbs 19:23

Honoring God

Them that honor me, I will honor. 1 Samuel 2:30

Honor the Lord with thy substance, and with the first-fruits of all thine increase. So shall thy barns be filled with plenty, and thy presses shall burst out with new wine.
          Proverbs 3:9–10

8. TO PRAYER

The Lord is nigh unto all them that call upon him, to all that call upon him in truth.   Psalm 145:18

I will call upon the Lord, who is worthy to be praised: so shall I be saved from mine enemies.   Psalm 18:3

He shall pray unto God, and he will be favorable unto him, and he shall see his face with joy.   Job 33:26

LORD, thou hast heard the desire of the humble: thou wilt prepare their heart, thou wilt cause thine ear to hear.
PSALM 10:17

Neither shall any man desire thy land, when thou shalt go up to appear before the LORD thy God, thrice in the year.
EXODUS 34:24

What nation is there so great, who hath God so nigh unto them, as the LORD our God is in all things that we call upon him for?
DEUTERONOMY 4:7

Thou, Lord, art good, and ready to forgive, and plenteous in mercy unto all them that call upon thee. In the day of my trouble, I will call upon thee, for thou wilt answer me.
PSALM 86:5, 7

It is good for me to draw near to God. PSALM 73:28

Draw nigh to God, and he will draw nigh to you.
JAMES 4:8

Whosoever shall call on the name of the LORD, shall be delivered.
JOEL 2:32

The LORD hath heard my supplication; the LORD will receive my prayer.
PSALM 6:9

Call unto me, and I will answer thee, and show thee great and mighty things, which thou knowest not.
JEREMIAH 33:3

I will yet for this be inquired of by the house of Israel, to do it for them; I will increase them with men like a flock.   EZEKIEL 36:37

Seeing then that we have a great high priest, that is passed into the heavens, Jesus the Son of God, let us hold fast our profession. For we have not an high priest which cannot be touched with the feeing of our infirmities; but was in all points tempted like as we are, yet without sin. Let us therefore come boldly unto the throne of grace, that we may obtain mercy, and find grace to help in time of need.   HEBREWS 4:14–16

Evening, and morning, and at noon, will I pray, and cry aloud; and he shall hear my voice.   PSALM 55:17

Acquaint now thyself with him, and be at peace; thereby good shall come unto thee.   JOB 22:21

The same Lord over all is rich unto all that call upon him. For whosoever shall call upon the name of the Lord shall be saved.   ROMANS 10:12–13

Seeking God

If thou seek him, he will be found of thee.
                                        1 CHRONICLES 28:9

Ye shall seek me and find me, when ye shall search for me with all your heart.   JEREMIAH 29:13

If from thence thou shalt seek the LORD thy God, thou shalt find him; if thou seek him with all thy heart, and with all thy soul.   DEUTERONOMY 4:29

If thou wouldest seek unto God betimes, and make thy supplication to the Almighty; if thou were pure and upright, surely now he would awake for thee, and make the habitation of thy righteousness prosperous.
                                                JOB 8:5–6

Seek ye me, and ye shall live.   AMOS 5:4

Your heart shall live, that seek God.   PSALM 69:32

Thou, LORD, hast not forsaken them that seek thee.
                                                PSALM 9:10

I said not unto the seed of Jacob, Seek ye me in vain.
                                                ISAIAH 45:19

The hand of our God is upon all them for good that seek him.   EZRA 8:22

Seek the LORD, till he come and rain righteousness upon you.   HOSEA 10:12

The LORD is good unto them that wait for him, to the soul that seeketh him.   LAMENTATIONS 3:25

That they should seek the Lord, if haply they might feel after him, and find him.   ACTS 17:27

The LORD is with you, while ye be with him; and if ye seek him, he will be found of you. 2 CHRONICLES 15:2

He that cometh to God must believe that he is, and that he is a rewarder of them that diligently seek him.
HEBREWS 11:6

Secret Prayer

Thou, when thou prayest, enter into thy closet, and when thou hast shut thy door, pray to thy Father which is in secret; and thy Father which seeth in secret, shall reward thee openly. MATTHEW 6:6

Praising God

Praise the LORD, for the LORD is good; sing praises unto his name, for it is pleasant. PSALM 135:3

I will praise the name of God with a song, and will magnify him with thanksgiving; this also shall please the LORD better than an ox or bullock that hath horns and hoofs. PSALM 69:30–31

It is a good thing to give thanks unto the LORD, and to sing praises unto thy name, O Most High; to show forth thy lovingkindness in the morning, and thy faithfulness every night. PSALM 92:1–2

Desires of Grace

Open thy mouth wide, and I will fill it. PSALM 81:10

I am Alpha and Omega, the beginning and the end: I will give unto him that is athirst, of the fountain of the water of life freely.   REVELATION 21:6

Blessed are they which do hunger and thirst after righteousness; for they shall be filled.   MATTHEW 5:6

And let him that is athirst come; and whosoever will, let him take the water of life freely.
     REVELATION 22:17

Ho, every one that thirsteth, come ye to the waters, and he that hath no money: come ye, buy and eat; yea, come, buy wine and milk without money and without price.   ISAIAH 55:1

Jesus stood and cried, saying, If any man thirst, let him come unto me and drink. He that believeth on me, as the scripture hath said, out of his belly shall flow rivers of living water.   JOHN 7:37–38

9. TO WISDOM AND KNOWLEDGE

To the Wise

Whoso findeth me [wisdom], findeth life, and shall obtain favor of the LORD.   PROVERBS 8:35

A wise man will hear, and will increase learning; and a man of understanding shall attain unto wise counsels: to understand a proverb, and the interpretation; the words of the wise and their dark sayings.
     PROVERBS 1:5–6

Good understanding giveth favor. PROVERBS 13:15

If thou be wise, thou shalt be wise for thyself.
PROVERBS 9:12

He is in the way of life, that keepeth instruction; but he that refuseth reproof, erreth.   PROVERBS 10:17

Forsake her not, and she shall preserve thee; love her, and she shall keep thee. Exalt her, and she shall promote thee: she shall bring thee to honour, when thou dost embrace her. She shall give to thy head an ornament of grace; a crown of glory shall she deliver to thee.
PROVERBS 4:6, 8–9

Happy is the man that findeth wisdom, and the man that getteth understanding; for the merchandise of it is better than the merchandise of silver, and the gain thereof than fine gold. She is more precious than rubies; and all the things thou canst desire, are not to be compared unto her. Length of days is in her right hand; and in her left hand riches and honour. Her ways are ways of pleasantness, and all her paths are peace. She is a tree of life to them that lay hold upon her; and happy is every one that retaineth her. The wise shall inherit glory.
PROVERBS 3:13–18, 35

The fool shall be servant to the wise of heart.
PROVERBS 11:29

There is treasure to be desired, and oil in the dwelling of the wise.   PROVERBS 21:20

He that getteth wisdom, loveth his own soul: he that keepeth understanding, shall find good. PROVERBS 19:8

He that handleth a matter wisely, shall find good. Understanding is a wellspring of life to him that hath it.
PROVERBS 16:20, 22

Wisdom is a defence, and money is a defence, but the excellency of knowledge is that wisdom giveth life to them that have it. ECCLESIASTES 7:12

Through wisdom is a house builded, and by understanding it is established: and by knowledge shall the chambers be filled with all precious and pleasant riches. A wise man is strong; yea, a man of knowledge increaseth strength. My son, eat thou honey, because it is good; and the honeycomb, which is sweet to thy taste: so shall the knowledge of wisdom be unto the soul: when thou hast found it, then there shall be a reward, and thy expectation shall not be cut off. PROVERBS 24:3–5, 13–14

Wisdom is profitable to direct. ECCLESIASTES 10:10

Whoso walketh wisely, he shall be delivered.
PROVERBS 28:26

A man shall be commended according to his wisdom.
PROVERBS 12:8

The way of life is above to the wise, that he may depart from hell beneath. PROVERBS 15:24

A man's wisdom maketh his face to shine, and the boldness of his face shall be changed.

ECCLESIASTES 8:1

He giveth wisdom unto the wise, and knowledge to them that know understanding.   DANIEL 2:21

Who is wise, and he shall understand these things? prudent, and he shall know them?   HOSEA 14:9

They that be wise shall shine as the brightness of the firmament. The wise shall understand.

DANIEL 12:3, 10

Whoso is wise, and will observe these things, even they shall understand the loving-kindness of the Lord.

PSALM 107:43

Love and Study of Wisdom

Then shall we know, if we follow on to know the Lord.

HOSEA 6:3

I love them that love me, and those that seek me early shall find me.   PROVERBS 8:17

Take fast hold of instruction; let her not go: keep her, for she is thy life.   PROVERBS 4:13

Hear counsel, and receive instruction, that thou mayest be wise in the latter end.   PROVERBS 19:20

If thou criest after knowledge, and liftest up thy voice for understanding; if thou seekest her as silver, and searchest for her as for hid treasures; then shalt thou understand the fear of the LORD, and find the knowledge of God.   PROVERBS 2:3–5

And God said to Solomon, Because this was in thy heart, and thou hast not asked riches, wealth, or honor, nor the life of thine enemies, neither yet hast asked long life; but hast asked wisdom and knowledge for thyself, that thou mayest judge my people, over whom I have made thee king: wisdom and knowledge is granted unto thee; and I will give thee riches and wealth and honor.
                    2 CHRONICLES 1:11–12

Knowledge of God and Christ

I will set him on high, because he hath known my name.   PSALM 91:14

And this is life eternal, that they might know thee, the only true God, and Jesus Christ whom thou hast sent.
                    JOHN 17:3

Grace and peace be multiplied unto you, through the knowledge of God, and of Jesus our Lord. According as his divine power hath given unto us all things that pertain unto life and godliness, through the knowledge of him that hath called us to glory and virtue.   2 PETER 1:2–3

Learning of Christ

Take my yoke upon you, and learn of me, for I am meek and lowly in heart; and ye shall find rest unto your souls.   MATTHEW 11:29

10. TO A DUE REGARD
TO THE WORD OF GOD

To Hearing and Reading the Word

Blessed is the man that heareth me, watching daily at my gates, waiting at the posts of my doors.
PROVERBS 8:34

Come ye, and let us go up to the mountain of the LORD, to the house of the God of Jacob, and he will teach us his ways, and we will walk in his paths. ISAIAH 2:3

It pleased God, by the foolishness of preaching, to save them that believe.   1 CORINTHIANS 1:21

Search the Scriptures, for in them ye think ye have eternal life; and they are they which testify of me.
JOHN 5:39

Unto you that hear, shall more be given. For he that hath, to him shall be given; and he that hath not, from him shall be taken even that which he hath.
MARK 4:24–25

Hearken diligently unto me, and eat ye that which is good, and let your soul delight itself in fatness. Incline your ear, and come unto me; hear, and your soul shall live; and I will make an everlasting covenant with you, even the sure mercies of David. For as the rain cometh down and the snow from heaven, and returneth not thither, but watereth the earth, and maketh it bring forth and bud, that it may give seed to the sower and bread to the eater; so shall my word be, that goeth forth out of my mouth; it shall not return unto me void, but it shall accomplish that which I please, and it shall prosper in the thing whereto I sent it. For ye shall go out with joy, and be led forth with peace.   Isaiah 55:2–3, 10–12

Faith cometh by hearing, and hearing by the word of God.   Romans 10:17

Blessed is he that readeth, and they that hear the words of this prophecy, and keep those things which are written therein.   Revelation 1:3

I am not ashamed of the gospel of Christ; for it is the power of God unto salvation, to every one that believeth.
                                                    Romans 1:16

Wherefore lay apart all filthiness and superfluity of naughtiness, and receive with meekness the ingrafted word, which is able to save your souls.   James 1:21

We have also a more sure word of prophecy; whereunto ye do well that ye take heed, as unto a light that shineth in a dark place, until the day dawn and the day star arise in your hearts.   2 Peter 1:19

The law of the LORD is perfect, converting the soul; the testimony of the LORD is sure, making wise the simple. The statutes of the LORD are right, rejoicing the heart; the commandment of the LORD is pure, enlightening the eyes. Moreover, by them is thy servant warned; and in keeping of them there is great reward.

PSALM 19:7–8, 11

The commandment is a lamp, and the law is a light, and reproofs of instruction are the way of life.

PROVERBS 6:23

The holy Scriptures which are able to make thee wise unto salvation, through faith which is in Christ Jesus.

2 TIMOTHY 3:15

Thy word is a lamp unto my feet, and a light unto my path. The entrance of thy words giveth light; it giveth understanding unto the simple.   PSALM 119:105, 130

For the word of God is quick and powerful, and sharper than any two-edged sword, piercing even to the dividing asunder of soul and spirit, and of the joints and marrow, and is a discerner of the thoughts and intents of the heart.   HEBREWS 4:12

Loving the Word

Great peace have they which love thy law, and nothing shall offend them.   PSALM 119:165

As newborn babes, desire the sincere milk of the word, that ye may grow thereby.   1 PETER 2:2

Blessed is the man that feareth the Lord, that delighteth greatly in his commandments.   PSALM 112:1

Trembling at the Word

He that feareth the commandment shall be rewarded.
          PROVERBS 13:13

To this man will I look, even to him that is poor, and of a contrite spirit, and trembleth at my word.
          ISAIAH 66:2

11. MEDITATION

Mercy and truth shall be to them that devise good.
          PROVERBS 14:22

The law of his God is in his heart; none of his steps shall slide.   PSALM 37:31

This book of the law shall not depart out of thy mouth, but thou shalt meditate therein day and night, that thou mayest observe to do according to all that is written therein; for then thou shalt make thy way prosperous, and then thou shalt have good success.   JOSHUA 1:8

Ye shall lay up these my words in your heart and in your soul, and bind them for a sign upon your hand, that they may be as frontlets between your eyes; that your days may be multiplied, and the days of your children, in the land which the LORD sware unto your fathers to give them, as the days of heaven upon the earth.

DEUTERONOMY 11:18, 21

Wherewith shall a young man cleanse his way? By taking heed thereto, according to thy word.

PSALM 119:9

Thou meetest him that rejoiceth and worketh righteousness, those that remember thee in thy ways.

ISAIAH 64:5

Ponder the path of thy feet, and let all thy ways be established [or, all thy ways shall be ordered aright].

PROVERBS 4:26

My soul shall be satisfied as with marrow and fatness, and my mouth shall praise thee with joyful lips; when I remember thee upon my bed, and meditate on thee in the night watches. PSALM 63:5–6

The mercy of the LORD is from everlasting to everlasting upon them that fear him, and his righteousness unto children's children; to such as keep his covenant, and to those that remember his commandment to do them. PSALM 103:17–18

His delight is in the law of the LORD, and in his law doth he meditate day and night. And he shall be like a tree planted by the rivers of water, that bringeth forth his fruit in his season: his leaf also shall not wither, and whatsoever he doeth shall prosper. PSALM 1:2–3

12. TO FASTING

Blow the trumpet in Zion, sanctify a fast, call a solemn assembly: gather the people, sanctify the congregation, assemble the elders, gather the children, and those that suck the breasts; let the bridegroom go forth of his chamber, and the bride out of her closet: let the priests, the ministers of the LORD, weep between the porch and the altar, and let them say, Spare thy people, O LORD, etc. Then will the LORD be jealous for his land, and pity his people.   JOEL 2:15–18

Fasting in Secret

Thou, when thou fastest, anoint thy head, and wash thy face, that thou appear not unto men to fast, but unto thy Father which is in secret; and thy Father which seeth in secret shall reward thee openly. MATTHEW 6:17–18

13. TO BAPTISM

He that believeth and is baptized shall be saved.
                                        MARK 16:16

Repent, and be baptized every one of you in the name of Jesus Christ for the remission of sins, and ye shall receive the gift of the Holy Ghost.   ACTS 2:38

For as many of you as have been baptized into Christ have put on Christ.   GALATIANS 3:27

Arise, and be baptized, and wash away thy sins, calling on the name of the Lord.   ACTS 22:16

By one Spirit are we all baptized into one body, whether we be Jews or Gentiles, whether we be bond or free.   1 CORINTHIANS 12:13

Buried with him in baptism, wherein also ye are risen with him through the faith of the operation of God, who hath raised him from the dead.   COLOSSIANS 2:12

Therein [that is, in the ark] few, that is, eight souls, were saved by water. The like figure whereunto even baptism doth also now save us, (not the putting away of the filth of the flesh, but the answer of a good conscience toward God), by the resurrection of Jesus Christ.
                                                    1 PETER 3:20–21

Know ye not, that so many of us as were baptized into Jesus Christ, were baptized into his death? Therefore, we are buried with him by baptism into death; that like as Christ was raised up from the dead by the glory of the Father, even so we also should walk in newness of life.   ROMANS 6:3–4

14. TO THE LORD'S SUPPER

We have been all made to drink into one Spirit.
                                                    1 CORINTHIANS 12:13

The cup of blessing which we bless, is it not the communion of the blood of Christ? The bread which we break, is it not the communion of the body of Christ?
                                                    1 CORINTHIANS 10:16

Jesus took bread, and blessed it, and brake it, and gave it to the disciples, and said, Take, eat; this is my body. And he took the cup, and gave thanks, and gave it to them, saying, Drink ye all of it; for this is my blood of the new testament, which is shed for many for the remission of sins.   MATTHEW 26:26–28

Whoso eateth my flesh, and drinketh my blood, hath eternal life; and I will raise him up at the last day. For my flesh is meat indeed, and my blood is drink indeed. He that eateth my flesh, and drinketh my blood, dwelleth in me, and I in him. As the living Father hath sent me, and I live by the Father; so he that eateth me, even he shall live by me. It is the spirit that quickeneth; the flesh profiteth nothing: the words that I speak unto you, they are spirit, and they are life.   JOHN 6:54–57, 63

Eat, O friends; drink, yea, drink abundantly, O beloved.   SONG OF SOLOMON 5:1

I sat down under his shadow with great delight, and his fruit was sweet to my taste. He brought me to the banqueting house, and his banner over me was love.
          SONG OF SOLOMON 2:3–4

And in this mountain shall the LORD of hosts make unto all people a feast of fat things, a feast of wines on the lees, of fat things full of marrow, of wines on the lees well refined.   ISAIAH 25:6

15. TO GOOD DISCOURSE

A wholesome tongue is a tree of life. A man hath joy by the answer of his mouth, and a word spoken in due season, how good is it!   PROVERBS 15:4, 23

Then they that feared the LORD spake often one to another, and the LORD hearkened and heard it: and a book of remembrance was written before him for them that feared the LORD, and that thought upon his name. And they shall be mine, saith the LORD of hosts, in that day when I make up my jewels; and I will spare them, as a man spareth his own son that serveth him.
                                        MALACHI 3:16–17

A man shall eat good by the fruit of his mouth.
                                        PROVERBS 13:2

Pleasant words are as a honeycomb, sweet to the soul, and health to the bones.   PROVERBS 16:24

A man's belly shall be satisfied with the fruit of his mouth; and with the increase of his lips shall he be filled. Death and life are in the power of the tongue and they that love it shall eat the fruit thereof.
                                        PROVERBS 18:20–21

The mouth of the upright shall deliver them. A man shall be satisfied with good by the fruit of his mouth: and the recompense of a man's hands shall be rendered unto him. The tongue of the wise is health.
                                        PROVERBS 12:6, 14, 18

The Government of the Tongue

The lips of the wise shall preserve them.

PROVERBS 14:3

Whoso keepeth his mouth and his tongue, keepeth his soul from troubles.   PROVERBS 21:23

He that will love life, and see good days, let him refrain his tongue from evil, and his lips that they speak no guile.   1 PETER 3:10

He that keepeth his mouth keepeth his life.

PROVERBS 13:3

By thy words thou shalt be justified, and by thy words thou shalt be condemned.   MATTHEW 12:37

16. TO WATCHFULNESS

Wherefore let him that thinketh he standeth take heed lest he fall.   1 CORINTHIANS 10:12

Happy is the man that feareth always; but he that hardeneth his heart shall fall into mischief.

PROVERBS 28:14

Watch ye therefore, lest coming suddenly, he find you sleeping; and what I say unto you, I say unto all, Watch.

MARK 13:35–37

Behold, I come as a thief. Blessed is he that watcheth, and keepeth his garments, lest he walk naked, and they see his shame.   REVELATION 16:15

Blessed are those servants, whom the Lord when he cometh shall find watching: . . . and will come forth and serve them. And if he shall come in the second watch, or come in the third watch, and find them so, blessed are those servants.   LUKE 12:37–38

17. TO KEEPING GOOD COMPANY

Iron sharpeneth iron; so a man sharpeneth the countenance of his friend.   PROVERBS 27:17

He that walketh with wise men shall be wise; but a companion of fools shall be destroyed.
                    PROVERBS 13:20

Avoiding Evil Company

Blessed is the man that walketh not in the counsel of the ungodly, nor standeth in the way of sinners, nor sitteth in the seat of the scornful.   PSALM 1:1

Come out from among them, and be ye separate, saith the Lord, and touch not the unclean thing, and I will receive you.   2 CORINTHIANS 6:17

18. TO PERFORMING OATHS

LORD, who shall abide in thy tabernacle? who shall dwell in thy holy hill? He that sweareth to his own hurt, and changeth not.   PSALM 15:1, 4

He who hath not lifted up his soul unto vanity, nor sworn deceitfully; he shall receive the blessing from the LORD, and righteousness from the God of his salvation.
                              PSALM 24:4–5

19. TO THE KEEPING OF THE SABBATH

The LORD blessed the Sabbath day, and hallowed it.
                              EXODUS 20:11

If thou turn away thy foot from the Sabbath, from doing thy pleasure on my holy day; and call the Sabbath a delight, the holy of the LORD, honorable; and shalt honor him, not doing thine own ways, nor finding thine own pleasure, not speaking thine own words: then shalt thou delight thyself in the LORD; and I will cause thee to ride upon the high places of the earth, and feed thee with the heritage of Jacob thy father; for the mouth of the LORD hath spoken it.   ISAIAH 58:13–14

Blessed is the man that doeth this, and the son of man that layeth hold on it; that keepeth the Sabbath from polluting it, and keepeth his hand from doing any evil. The sons of the stranger that join themselves to the LORD, to serve him, and to love the name of the LORD, to be his servants, every one that keepeth the Sabbath from polluting it, and taketh hold of my covenant; even them will I bring to my holy mountain, and make them joyful in my house of prayer: for my house shall be called a house of prayer for all people.   ISAIAH 56:2, 6–7

The Sabbath was made for man, and not man for the Sabbath.   MARK 2:27

This is the day which the LORD hath made; we will rejoice and be glad in it.   PSALM 118:24

Upon the first day of the week, when the disciples came together to break bread, Paul preached unto them.
ACTS 20:7

Hallow my Sabbaths; and they shall be a sign between me and you, that ye may know that I am the LORD your God.   EZEKIEL 20:20

The same day at evening, being the first day of the week, came Jesus and stood in the midst, and saith unto them, Peace be unto you.   JOHN 20:19

I was in the Spirit on the Lord's day, and heard behind me a great voice, as of a trumpet, saying, I am Alpha and Omega, the first and the last.
REVELATION 1:10–11

It shall come to pass, if ye diligently hearken unto me, saith the LORD, to hallow the Sabbath day, to do no work therein; then shall there enter into the gates of this city kings and princes sitting upon the throne of David.
JEREMIAH 17:24–25

Two

In the Performance of Duty toward Men

1. TO OBEDIENCE TO PARENTS

Children, obey your parents in the Lord; for this is right. Honor thy father and mother; which is the first commandment with promise; that it may be well with thee, and thou mayest live long on the earth.

EPHESIANS 6:1–3

My son, hear the instruction of thy father, and forsake not the law of thy mother; for they shall be an ornament of grace unto thy head, and chains about thy neck.

PROVERBS 1:8–9

But if any widow have children, or nephews [grandchildren], let them learn first to show piety at home, and to requite their parents; for that is good and acceptable before God.   1 TIMOTHY 5:5

Children, obey your parents in all things; for this is well-pleasing unto the Lord.   COLOSSIANS 3:20

My son, keep thy father's commandment, and forsake not the law of thy mother: bind them continually upon thy heart, and tie them about thy neck. When thou goest, it shall lead thee; when thou sleepest, it shall keep thee; and when thou awakest, it shall talk with thee.
                                        PROVERBS 6:20–22

Thus saith the LORD of hosts, the God of Israel: Because ye have obeyed the commandment of Jonadab your father, and kept all his precepts, and done according unto all that he hath commanded you; therefore thus saith the LORD of hosts, the God of Israel: Jonadab . . . shall not want a man to stand before me for ever.
                                        JEREMIAH 35:18–19

2. TO GOOD EDUCATION

For I know him [Abraham], that he will command his children and his household after him, and they shall keep the way of the LORD, to do justice and judgment, that the LORD may bring upon Abraham that which he hath spoken of him.   GENESIS 18:19

Train up a child in the way he should go; and when he is old, he will not depart from it.   PROVERBS 22:6

And ye shall teach these my words to your children, speaking of them when thou sittest in thine house, and when thou walkest by the way, when thou liest down, and when thou risest up. And thou shalt write them upon the door posts of thine house, and upon thy gates: that your days may be multiplied, and the days of your children, in the land which the LORD sware unto your fathers to give them, as the days of heaven upon the earth.

DEUTERONOMY 11:19–21

Correction of Children

Foolishness is bound in the heart of a child; but the rod of correction shall drive it far from him.

PROVERBS 22:15

Withhold not correction from the child: for if thou beatest him with the rod, he shall not die. Thou shalt beat him with the rod, and shalt deliver his soul from hell.

PROVERBS 23:13–14

The rod and reproof give wisdom; but a child left to himself bringeth his mother to shame. Correct thy son, and he shall give thee rest; yea, he shall give delight unto thy soul.

PROVERBS 29:15, 17

3. TO A GOOD WIFE

Every wise woman buildeth her house.

PROVERBS 14:1

A gracious woman retaineth honor: and strong men retain riches.   PROVERBS 11:16

A virtuous woman is a crown to her husband; but she that maketh ashamed is as rottenness in his bones.
                                                    PROVERBS 12:4

Who can find a virtuous woman? for her price is far above rubies. Strength and honor are her clothing; and she shall rejoice in time to come. Her children arise up, and call her blessed; her husband also, and he praiseth her. Favor is deceitful, and beauty is vain; but a woman that feareth the LORD, she shall be praised. Give her of the fruit of her hands; and let her own works praise her in the gates.   PROVERBS 31:10, 25, 28, 30–31

4. TO FAITHFUL SERVANTS

Whoso keepeth the fig-tree shall eat the fruit thereof; so he that waiteth on his master shall be honored.
                                                    PROVERBS 27:18

A wise servant shall have rule over a son that causeth shame, and shall have part of the inheritance among the brethren.   PROVERBS 17:2

The king's favor is toward a wise servant.
                                                    PROVERBS 14:35

Servants, obey in all things your masters according to the flesh, etc.; knowing that of the Lord ye shall receive

the reward of the inheritance; for ye serve the Lord
Christ. COLOSSIANS 3:22, 24

Servants, be obedient to them that are your masters
according to the flesh, with fear and trembling, in sin-
gleness of your heart, as unto Christ: not with eye-ser-
vice, as men-pleasers; but as the servants of Christ, doing
the will of God from the heart; with good-will doing ser-
vice, as to the Lord, and not to men: knowing that whatsoever good thing any man doeth, the same shall he
receive of the Lord, whether he be bond or free.
EPHESIANS 6:5–8

5. TO GOOD KINGS AND MAGISTRATES

The throne is established by righteousness.
PROVERBS 16:12

Mercy and truth preserve the king; and his throne is
upholden by mercy. PROVERBS 20:28

The king that faithfully judgeth the poor, his throne
shall be established for ever. PROVERBS 29:14

In that day shall the LORD of hosts be for a spirit of
judgment to him that sitteth in judgment, and for
strength to them that turn the battle to the gate.
ISAIAH 28:5–6

And it shall be, when he sitteth upon the throne of
his kingdom, that he shall write him a copy of this law
in a book out of that which is before the priests the

Levites: and it shall be with him, and he shall read therein all the days of his life; that he may learn to fear the LORD his God, to keep all the words of this law and these statutes, to do them: that his heart be not lifted up above his brethren, and that he turn not aside from the commandment, to the right hand, or to the left; to the end that he may prolong his days in his kingdom, he and his children, in the midst of Israel.

DEUTERONOMY 17:18–20

6. TO OBEDIENT SUBJECTS

Submit yourselves to every ordinance of man for the Lord's sake: whether it be to the king, as supreme; or unto governors, as unto them that are sent by him for the punishment of evildoers, and for the praise of them that do well. For so is the will of God, that with well-doing ye may put to silence the ignorance of foolish men.

1 PETER 2:13–15

Whoso keepeth the commandment [the king's] shall feel no evil thing; and a wise man's heart discerneth both time and judgment.   ECCLESIASTES 8:5

7. TO FAITHFUL MINISTERS

Then I said, I have labored in vain, I have spent my strength for naught, and in vain; yet surely my judgment is with the LORD, and my work with my God.

ISAIAH 49:4

Blessed are ye that sow beside all waters, that send forth thither the feet of the ox and the ass.   ISAIAH 32:20

And I will satiate the soul of the priests with fatness, and my people shall be satisfied with my goodness, saith the LORD.   JEREMIAH 31:14

The elders which are among you I exhort: feed the flock of God which is among you, taking the oversight thereof, not by constraint, but willingly; not for filthy lucre, but of a ready mind. Neither as being lords over God's heritage, but being ensamples to the flock. And when the chief Shepherd shall appear, ye shall receive a crown of glory that fadeth not away.   1 PETER 5:1–4

These things saith he that holdeth the seven stars in his right hand.   REVELATION 2:1

Take heed unto thyself, and unto the doctrine; continue in them: for in doing this thou shalt both save thyself and them that hear thee.   1 TIMOTHY 4:16

And they that be wise shall shine as the brightness of the firmament; and they that turn many to righteousness, as the stars for ever and ever.   DANIEL 12:3

Teaching them to observe all things whatsoever I have commanded you; and lo, I am with you alway, even unto the end of the world.   MATTHEW 28:20

And he that reapeth receiveth wages, and gathered fruit unto life eternal; that both he that soweth, and he that reapeth, may rejoice together.   JOHN 4:36

Who then is that faithful and wise steward, whom his Lord shall make ruler over his household, to give them their portion of meat in due season? Blessed is that servant, whom his Lord when he cometh shall find so doing. Of a truth I say unto you, that he will make him ruler over all that he hath. LUKE 12:42–44

I will clothe her priests with salvation; and her saints shall shout aloud for joy. PSALM 132:16

The LORD is with me as a mighty terrible one; therefore my persecutors shall stumble, and they shall not prevail: they shall be greatly ashamed, for they shall not prosper; their everlasting confusion shall never be forgotten. JEREMIAH 20:11

Behold, I have made thy face strong against their faces, and thy forehead strong against their foreheads. As an adamant harder than flint, have I made thy forehead: fear them not, neither be dismayed at their looks, though they be a rebellious house. EZEKIEL 3:8–9

Thus saith the LORD, If thou return, then will I bring thee again, and thou shalt stand before me; and if thou take forth the precious from the vile, thou shalt be as my mouth: let them return unto thee, but return not thou unto them. And I will make thee unto this people a fenced brazen wall; and they shall fight against thee, but they shall not prevail against thee, etc. And I will deliver thee out of the hand of the wicked, and I will redeem thee out of the hand of the terrible. JEREMIAH 15:19–21

I will give you a mouth and wisdom, which all your adversaries shall not be able to gainsay nor resist.
LUKE 21:15

Levi hath no part nor inheritance with his brethren; the LORD is his inheritance, according as the LORD thy God promised him.   DEUTERONOMY 10:9

Bless, LORD, his [Levi's] substance, and accept the work of his hands: smite through the loins of them that rise against him, and of them that hate him, that they rise not again.   DEUTERONOMY 33:11

When they deliver you up, take no thought how or what ye shall speak; for it shall be given you in that same hour what ye shall speak. For it is not ye that speak, but the Spirit of your Father which speaketh in you.
                    MATTHEW 10:19–20

The LORD said unto me, Say not, I am a child; for thou shalt go to all that I shall send thee, and whatsoever I command thee thou shalt speak. Be not afraid of their faces; for I am with thee to deliver thee, saith the LORD. They shall fight against thee; but they shall not prevail against thee; for I am with thee, saith the LORD, to deliver thee.   JEREMIAH 1:7–8, 19

8. TO THEM THAT RECEIVE AND HEARKEN TO MINISTERS

He that heareth you, heareth me.   LUKE 10:16

Believe in the LORD your God, so shall ye be established; believe his prophets, so shall ye prosper.
                    2 CHRONICLES 20:20

He that receiveth you, receiveth me; and he that receiveth me receiveth him that sent me. (See John 13:20.) He that receiveth a prophet in the name of a prophet, shall receive a prophet's reward; and he that receiveth a righteous man in the name of a righteous man, shall receive a righteous man's reward.

MATTHEW 10:40–41

9. TO LOVE AND UNITY

By this shall all men know that ye are my disciples, if ye have love one to another. JOHN 13:35

He that loveth his brother, abideth in the light, and there is none occasion of stumbling in him.

1 JOHN 2:10

Be perfect, be of good comfort, be of one mind, live in peace; and the God of love and peace shall be with you.

2 CORINTHIANS 13:11

Behold how good and how pleasant it is for brethren to dwell together in unity! It is like the precious ointment upon the head, that ran down upon the beard, even Aaron's beard; that went down to the skirts of his garments. As the dew of Hermon, and as the dew that descended upon the mountains of Zion; for there the LORD commanded the blessing, even life for evermore.

PSALM 133:1–3

To the Peacemakers

To the counsellors of peace is joy. PROVERBS 12:20

Blessed are the peacemakers; for they shall be called the children of God.   MATTHEW 5:9

He that will love life, and see good days, . . . let him seek peace, and ensue it.   1 PETER 3:10–11

Love to God's People

Pray for the peace of Jerusalem; they shall prosper that love thee.   PSALM 122:6

LORD, who shall abide in thy tabernacle? who shall dwell in thy holy hill? He in whose eyes a vile person is condemned; but he honoreth them that fear the LORD.
                                    PSALM 15:1, 4

If we love one another, God dwelleth in us, and his love is perfected in us.   1 JOHN 4:12

Blessed is he that blesseth thee, and cursed is he that curseth thee.   NUMBERS 24:9

God is not unrighteous to forget your work and labor of love, which ye have showed toward his name, in that ye have ministered to the saints, and do minister.
                                    HEBREWS 6:10

We know that we have passed from death unto life, because we love the brethren. He that loveth not his brother abideth in death. My little children, let us not love in word, neither in tongue; but in deed and in truth. And hereby we know that we are of the truth, and shall assure our hearts before him.   1 JOHN 3:14, 18–19

10. TO THE CHARITABLE, THE MERCIFUL, AND THE LIBERAL TO GOD'S MINISTERS

He that hath mercy on the poor, happy is he.
PROVERBS 14:21

He that hath pity upon the poor, lendeth unto the LORD; and that which he hath given will he pay him again.   PROVERBS 19:17

I have been young, and now am old; yet have I not seen the righteous forsaken, nor his seed begging bread. He is ever merciful, and lendeth; and his seed is blessed.
PSALM 37:25–26

There is that scattereth, and yet increaseth; and there is that withholdeth more than is meet, but it tendeth to poverty. The liberal soul shall be made fat; and he that watereth shall be watered also himself. He that diligently seeketh good, procureth favor. PROVERBS 11:24–25, 27

He hath dispersed, he hath given to the poor, his righteousness endureth for ever; his horn shall be exalted with honor. A good man showeth favor and lendeth: he will guide his affairs with discretion. Surely he shall not be moved for ever; the righteous shall be in everlasting remembrance.   PSALM 112:5–6, 9

Blessed is he that considereth the poor; the LORD will deliver him in time of trouble. The LORD will preserve him and keep him alive; and he shall be blessed upon the earth; and thou wilt not deliver him unto the will of his enemies. The LORD will strengthen him upon the bed of languishing; thou wilt make all his bed in his sickness.   PSALM 41:1–3

And whosoever shall give **to** drink unto one of these little ones a cup of cold water only in the name of a disciple, verily I say unto you, he shall in no wise lose his reward.   MATTHEW 10:42

Cast thy bread upon the waters; for thou shalt find it after many days. Give a portion to seven, and also to eight; for thou knowest not what evil shall be upon the earth.   ECCLESIASTES 11:1–2

Is it not [the fast that I have chosen] to deal thy bread to the hungry, and that thou bring the poor that are cast out to thy house? When thou seest the naked, that thou cover him; and that thou hide not thyself from thine own flesh? Then shall thy light break forth as the morning, and thy health shall spring forth speedily: and thy righteousness shall go before thee; the glory of the LORD shall be thy rearward. If thou draw out thy soul to the hungry, and satisfy the afflicted soul: then shall thy light rise in obscurity, and thy darkness be as the noonday; and the LORD shall guide thee continually, and satisfy thy soul in drought, and make fat thy bones; and thou shalt be like a watered garden, and like a spring of water, whose waters fail not.   ISAIAH 58:7–8, 10–11

The liberal deviseth liberal things, and by liberal things shall he stand   ISAIAH 32:8

He that hath a bountiful eye shall be blessed; for he giveth of his bread to the poor.   PROVERBS 22:9

He that by usury and unjust gain increaseth his substance, he shall gather it for him that will pity the poor. He that giveth unto the poor shall not lack.
PROVERBS 28:8, 27

And I say unto you, Make to yourselves friends of the mammon of unrighteousness; that when ye fail, they may receive you into everlasting habitations.
LUKE 16:9

Then shall the King say unto them on his right hand, Come, ye blessed of my Father, inherit the kingdom prepared for you from the foundation of the world: for I was a-hungered, and ye gave me meat: I was thirsty, and ye gave me drink: I was a stranger, and ye took me in: naked, and ye clothed me: I was sick, and ye visited me: I was in prison, and ye came unto me. Verily, I say unto you, Inasmuch as ye have done it unto one of the least of these my brethren, ye have done it unto me.
MATTHEW 25:34–36, 40

Give alms of such things as ye have; and behold, all things are clean unto you.   LUKE 11:41

Sell that ye have, and give alms; provide yourselves bags which wax not old, a treasure in the heavens, that faileth not, where no thief approacheth, neither moth corrupteth.   LUKE 12:33

When thou makest a feast, call the poor, the maimed, the lame, the blind: and thou shalt be blessed; for they cannot recompense thee: for thou shalt be recompensed at the resurrection of the just.   LUKE 14:13–14

Give, and it shall be given unto you; good measure, pressed down, and shaken together and running over, shall men give into your bosom. For with the same measure that ye mete withal, it shall be measured to you again.   LUKE 6:38

God is able to make all grace abound toward you; that ye, always having all sufficiency in all things, may abound to every good work. Now he that ministereth seed to the sower both minister bread for your food, and multiply your seed sown, and increase the fruits of your righteousness.   2 CORINTHIANS 9:8, 10

To do good and to communicate forget not; for with such sacrifices God is well pleased.   HEBREWS 13:16

Go thy way, sell whatsoever thou hast, and give to the poor, and thou shalt have treasure in heaven.
                                               MARK 10:21

If there be first a willing mind, it is accepted according to that a man hath, and not according to that he hath not.   2 CORINTHIANS 8:12

He which soweth sparingly shall reap also sparingly; and he which soweth bountifully shall reap also bountifully. God loveth a cheerful giver.

2 CORINTHIANS 9:6–7

Thou shalt surely give him [thy poor brother], and thy heart shall not be grieved when thou givest unto him; because that for this thing the LORD thy God shall bless thee in all thy works, and in all that thou puttest thy hand unto.

DEUTERONOMY 15:10

Charge them that are rich in this world, that they do good, that they be rich in good works, ready to distribute, willing to communicate, laying up in store for themselves a good foundation against the time to come, that they may lay hold on eternal life. 1 TIMOTHY 6:17–19

To Alms in Secret

When thou doest alms, let not thy left hand know what thy right hand doeth; that thine alms may be in secret: and thy Father which seeth in secret, himself shall reward thee openly.

MATTHEW 6:3–4

To the Supporting of God's Ministers and Worship

Honor the LORD with thy substance, and with the first-fruits of all thine increase; so shall thy barns be filled with plenty, and thy presses shall burst out with new wine.

PROVERBS 3:9–10

And the Levite, because he hath no part nor inheritance with thee, and the stranger, and the fatherless, and the widow, which are within thy gates, shall come, and shall eat and be satisfied; that the LORD thy God may bless thee in all the work of thy hand which thou doest.

DEUTERONOMY 14:29

Bring ye all the tithes into the storehouse, that there may be meat in my house, and prove me now herewith, saith the LORD of hosts, if I will not open you the windows of heaven, and pour you out a blessing, that there shall not be room enough to receive it. And I will rebuke the devourer for your sakes, and he shall not destroy the fruits of your ground; neither shall your vine cast her fruit before the time in the field, saith the LORD of hosts. And all nations shall call you blessed; for ye shall be a delightsome land, saith the LORD of hosts.

MALACHI 3:10–12

Let him that is taught in the word, communicate unto him that teacheth in all good things. Be not deceived; God is not mocked; for whatsoever a man soweth, that shall he also reap. For he that soweth to his flesh shall of the flesh reap corruption; but he that soweth to the Spirit shall of the Spirit reap life everlasting.

GALATIANS 6:6–8

Not because I desire a gift; but I desire fruit that may abound to your account. But I have all, and abound; I am full, having received of Epaphroditus the things which were sent from you, an odor of a sweet smell, a sacrifice acceptable, well pleasing to God. But my God shall supply all your need according to his riches in glory by Christ Jesus. PHILIPPIANS 4:17–19

To the Merciful

The merciful man doeth good to his own soul; but he that is cruel troubleth his own flesh. PROVERBS 11:17

Blessed are the merciful, for they shall obtain mercy.
MATTHEW 5:7

With the merciful, thou wilt show thyself merciful.
PSALM 18:25

Let no mercy and truth forsake thee; bind them about thy neck, write them upon the table of thy heart. So shalt thou find favor and good understanding in the sight of God and man. PROVERBS 3:3–4

If the man be poor, thou shalt not sleep with his pledge. In any case thou shalt deliver him the pledge again when the sun goeth down, that he may sleep in his own raiment, and bless thee; and it shall be righteousness unto thee before the LORD thy God.
DEUTERONOMY 24:12–13

11. TO THE GIVING AND THE RECEIVING OF REPROOFS

To them that rebuke him [the wicked] shall be delight, and a good blessing shall come upon them.
PROVERBS 24:25

He that rebuketh a man, afterwards shall find more favor than he that flattereth with the tongue.

PROVERBS 28:23

Poverty and shame shall be to him that refuseth instruction, but he that regardeth reproof shall be honored.

PROVERBS 13:18

As an earring of gold, and an ornament of fine gold, so is a wise reprover upon an obedient ear.

PROVERBS 25:12

The ear that heareth the reproof of life abideth among the wise. He that refuseth instruction despiseth his own soul; but he that heareth reproof getteth understanding.

PROVERBS 15:31–32

12. TO FORGIVING INJURIES

Say not thou, I will recompense evil; but wait on the LORD, and he shall save thee.   PROVERBS 20:22

Love ye your enemies, and do good, and lend, hoping for nothing again; and your reward shall be great, and ye shall be the children of the Highest: for he is kind unto the unthankful and to the evil. Forgive, and ye shall be forgiven.   LUKE 6:35, 37

Love your enemies, bless them that curse you, do good to them that hate you, and pray for them which despitefully use you and persecute you; that ye may be the children of your Father which is in heaven: for he maketh his sun to rise on the evil and on the good, and sendeth rain on the just and the unjust.

MATTHEW 5:44–45

If ye forgive men their trespasses, your heavenly Father will also forgive you. MATTHEW 6:14

And when ye stand praying, forgive, if ye have aught against any; that your Father also, which is in heaven, may forgive you your trespasses. MARK 11:25

Not rendering evil for evil, or railing for railing; but contrariwise, blessing; knowing that ye are thereunto called, that ye should inherit a blessing. 1 PETER 3:9

If thine enemy be hungry, give him bread to eat; and if he be thirsty, give him water to drink; for thou shall heap coals of fire upon his head, and the Lord shall reward thee. PROVERBS 25:21–22; SEE ROMANS 12:20

13. TO CHASTITY AND PURITY

Blessed are the pure in heart; for they shall see God.

MATTHEW 5:8

If a man be just, and do that which is lawful and right; and hath not defiled his neighbor's wife, neither hath come near to a menstruous woman; hath walked in my statutes, and hath kept my judgments, to deal truly; he is just, he shall surely live, saith the Lord GOD.

EZEKIEL 18:5–6, 9

Unto the pure all things are pure. TITUS 1:15

With the pure thou wilt show thyself pure.

PSALM 18:26

Truly God is good to Israel, even to such as are of a clean heart. PSALM 73:1

Who shall ascend into the hill of the LORD? or who shall stand in his holy place? He that hath clean hands, and a pure heart. PSALM 24:3–4

If a man therefore purge himself from these, he shall be a vessel unto honor, sanctified, and meet for the Master's use, and prepared unto every good work.

2 TIMOTHY 2:21

14. TO DILIGENCE

The hand of the diligent maketh rich.

PROVERBS 10:4

In all labor there is profit; but the talk of the lips tendeth only to penury. PROVERBS 14:23

The soul of the sluggard desireth, and hath nothing: but the soul of the diligent shall be made fat. Wealth gotten by vanity shall be diminished; but he that gathereth by labor shall increase. PROVERBS 13:4, 11

The thoughts of the diligent tend only to plenteousness; but of every one that is hasty, only to want.

PROVERBS 21:5

Seest thou a man diligent in his business? he shall stand before kings; he shall not stand before mean men.
PROVERBS 22:29

He that tilleth his land shall have plenty of bread; but he that followeth after vain persons shall have poverty enough.
PROVERBS 28:19

The hand of the diligent shall bear rule; but the slothful shall be under tribute. The substance of a diligent man is precious. He that tilleth his land shall be satisfied with bread.
PROVERBS 12:11, 24, 27

To Improving Our Talents

Well done, good and faithful servant; thou hast been faithful over a few things, I will make thee ruler over many things: enter thou into the joy of thy Lord. Unto every one that hath shall be given, and he shall have abundance.
MATTHEW 13:12; 25:23, 29

Moderation in Sleep

Love not sleep, lest thou come to poverty; open thine eyes, and thou shalt be satisfied with bread.
PROVERBS 20:13

15. TO THE JUST AND HONEST

He that is greedy of gain troubleth his own house; but he that hateth gifts shall live.
PROVERBS 15:27

A false balance is abomination to the LORD; but a just weight is his delight.   PROVERBS 11:1

There shall no evil happen to the just; but the wicked shall be filled with mischief.   PROVERBS 12:21

A faithful man shall abound with blessings; but he that maketh haste to be rich shall not be innocent.
                                                   PROVERBS 28:20

That which is altogether just shalt thou follow, that thou mayest live, and inherit the land which the LORD thy God giveth thee.   DEUTERONOMY 16:20

He that walketh righteously, and speaketh uprightly; he that despiseth the gain of oppressions, that shaketh his hand from holding of bribes, that stoppeth his ears from hearing of blood, and shutteth his eyes from seeing evil; he shall dwell on high; his place of defence shall be the munitions of rocks: bread shall be given him; his waters shall be sure.   ISAIAH 33:15–16

Better is a little with righteousness, than great revenues without right.   PROVERBS 16:8

To do justice and judgment is more acceptable to the LORD than sacrifice.   PROVERBS 21:3

He that putteth not out his money to usury, nor taketh reward against the innocent; he that doeth these things, shall never be moved.   PSALM 15:5

Thou shalt have a perfect and just weight, a perfect and just measure shalt thou have; that thy days may be lengthened in the land which the LORD thy God giveth thee. DEUTERONOMY 25:15

If a man be just, and do that which is lawful and right, and hath not oppressed any, but hath restored to the debtor his pledge, hath spoiled none by violence, hath given his bread to the hungry, and hath covered the naked with a garment: he that hath not given forth upon usury, neither hath taken any increase, that hath withdrawn his hand from iniquity, hath executed true judgment between man and man, hath walked in my statutes, and hath kept my judgments, to deal truly; he is just, he shall surely live, saith the Lord GOD. EZEKIEL 18:5, 7–9

Thus saith the LORD, Keep ye judgment, and do justice; for my salvation is near to come, and my righteousness to be revealed. Blessed is the man that doeth this, and the son of man that layeth hold on it.
ISAIAH 56:1–2

16. TO TRUTH

He that will love life, and see good days, let him refrain his tongue from evil, and his lips that they speak no guile. 1 PETER 3:10; SEE PSALM 34:12–13

The lip of truth shall be established for ever; but a lying tongue is but for a moment. Lying lips are abomination to the LORD; but they that deal truly are his delight. PROVERBS 12:19, 22

Lord, who shall abide in thy tabernacle? Who shall dwell in thy holy hill? He that speaketh the truth in his heart. He that backbiteth not with his tongue, nor doeth evil to his neighbour.   Psalm 15:1–3

17. TO CANDOR

Judge not, that ye be not judged. For with what judgment ye judge, ye shall be judged; and with what measure ye mete, it shall be measured to you again.
                                        Matthew 7:1–2

Lord, who shall abide, etc. He that backbiteth not with his tongue, nor doeth evil to his neighbour, nor taketh up a reproach against his neighbour.   Psalm 15:1, 3

18. TO CONTENTMENT AND MORTIFICATION

Contentment

Godliness with contentment is great gain.
                                        1 Timothy 6:6

A sound heart is the life of the flesh, but envy the rottenness of the bones.   Proverbs 14:30

A merry heart doeth good like a medicine; but a broken spirit drieth the bones.   Proverbs 17:22

All the days of the afflicted are evil; but he that is of a merry heart hath a continual feast. Proverbs 15:15

Let your conversation be without covetousness, and be content with such things as ye have; for he hath said, I will never leave thee, nor forsake thee.

HEBREWS 13:5

Let not thy heart envy sinners; but be thou in the fear of the LORD all the day long. For surely there is an end, and thine expectation shall not be cut off.

PROVERBS 23:17–18

Mortification of Sin

If ye through the Spirit do mortify the deeds of the body, ye shall live. ROMANS 8:13

If thy right eye offend thee, pluck it out, and cast it from thee; for it is profitable for thee that one of thy members should perish, and not that thy whole body should be cast into hell. And if thy right hand offend thee, cut it off, and cast it from thee; for it is profitable for thee that one of thy members should perish, and not that thy whole body should be cast into hell.

MATTHEW 5:29–30

To the Spiritually Minded

To be carnally-minded is death; but to be spiritually-minded is life and peace. ROMANS 8:6

Three

In the Cultivation of Christian Character

1. TO THE MEEK, HUMBLE, CONTRITE

The Meek

Seek ye the L ORD, all ye meek of the earth, which have wrought his judgment; seek righteousness, seek meekness: it may be ye shall be hid in the day of the Lord's anger.   Z EPHANIAH 2:3

A soft answer turneth away wrath. He that is slow to anger appeaseth strife.   P ROVERBS 15:1, 18

Whose adorning, let it not be that outward adorning of plaiting the hair, and of wearing of gold, or of putting on of apparel: but let it be the hidden man of the heart, in that which is not corruptible: even the ornament of a meek and quiet spirit, which is in the sight of God of great price.   1 PETER 3:3–4

He that is slow to wrath is of great understanding.
                                                        PROVERBS 14:29

Blessed are the meek; for they shall inherit the earth.
                                                        MATTHEW 5:5

The meek will he guide in judgment, and the meek will he teach his way.   PSALM 25:9

The LORD lifteth up the meek: he casteth the wicked down to the ground   PSALM 147:6

The LORD taketh pleasure in his people; he will beautify the meek with salvation.   PSALM 149:4

The meek shall inherit the earth, and shall delight themselves in the abundance of peace   PSALM 37:11

With righteousness shall he judge the poor, and reprove with equity for the meek of the earth.
                                                        ISAIAH 11:4

The meek shall eat and be satisfied; they shall praise the LORD that seek him; your heart shall live for ever.
                                                        PSALM 22:26

The meek shall increase their joy in the LORD, and the poor among men shall rejoice in the Holy One of Israel.   ISAIAH 29:19

It is an honor for a man to cease from strife.
PROVERBS 20:3

The discretion of a man deferreth his anger, and it is his glory to pass over a transgression. PROVERBS 19:11

He that is slow to anger is better than the mighty; and he that ruleth his spirit, than he that taketh a city.
PROVERBS 16:32

The Humble

He shall save the humble person.   JOB 22:29

He forgetteth not the cry of the humble.
PSALM 9:12

Lord, thou hast heard the desire of the humble.
PSALM 10:17

Surely he scorneth the scorners; but he giveth grace unto the lowly.   PROVERBS 3:34

When pride cometh, then cometh shame; but with the lowly is wisdom.   PROVERBS 11:2

Wherefore he saith, God resisteth the proud, but giveth grace unto the humble. JAMES 4:6; 1 PETER 5:5

Though the LORD be high, yet hath he respect unto the lowly; but the proud he knoweth afar off.
PSALM 138:6

By humility, and the fear of the LORD, are riches, and honor, and life. PROVERBS 22:4

A man's pride shall bring him low; but honor shall uphold the humble in spirit. PROVERBS 29:23

The fear of the LORD is the instruction of wisdom; and before honor is humility. PROVERBS 15:33

Before destruction the heart of man is haughty; and before honor is humility. PROVERBS 18:12

Better it is to be of a humble spirit with the lowly, than to divide the spoil with the proud. PROVERBS 16:19

Whosoever shall humble himself as this little child, the same is greatest in the kingdom of heaven.
MATTHEW 18:4

Whosoever shall exalt himself shall be abased; and he that shall humble himself shall be exalted.
MATTHEW 23:12; LUKE 18:14

The Contrite and Mourners

The LORD is nigh unto them that are of a broken heart, and saveth such as be of a contrite spirit. PSALM 34:18

He healeth the broken in heart, and bindeth up their wounds. PSALM 147:3

Sorrow is better than laughter; for by the sadness of the countenance the heart is made better.

ECCLESIASTES 7:3

To this man will I look, even to him that is poor, and of a contrite spirit, and trembleth at my word.

ISAIAH 66:2

The sacrifices of God are a broken spirit; a broken and a contrite heart, O God, thou wilt not despise.

PSALM 51:17

Blessed are the poor in spirit; for theirs is the kingdom of heaven. Blessed are they that mourn; for they shall be comforted.   MATTHEW 5:3–4

Thus saith the high and lofty One that inhabiteth eternity, whose name is Holy. I dwell in the high and holy place, with him also that is of a contrite and humble spirit, to revive the spirit of the humble, and to revive the heart of the contrite ones.   ISAIAH 57:15

2. TO THEM THAT SUFFER FOR RIGHTEOUSNESS' SAKE

He that findeth his life shall lose it; and he that loseth his life for my sake, shall find it.   MATTHEW 10:39

If we suffer, we shall also reign with him.

2 TIMOTHY 2:12

Every one that hath forsaken houses, or brethren, or sisters, or father, or mother, or wife, or children, or lands, for my name's sake, shall receive a hundredfold, and shall inherit everlasting life.   MATTHEW 19:29

Blessed are they which are persecuted for righteousness' sake; for theirs is the kingdom of heaven. Blessed are ye when men shall revile you, and persecute you, and shall say all manner of evil against you falsely, for my sake. Rejoice, and be exceeding glad, for great is your reward in heaven; for so persecuted they the prophets which were before you.   MATTHEW 5:10–12

If so be that we suffer with him, that we may be also glorified together. Who shall separate us from the love of Christ? Shall tribulation, or distress, or persecution, or famine, or nakedness, or peril, or sword? As it is written, For thy sake we are killed all the day long; we are accounted as sheep for the slaughter. Nay, in all these things we are more than conquerors through him that loved us.   ROMANS 8:17, 35–37

Persecuted, but not forsaken.   2 CORINTHIANS 4:9

If ye suffer for righteousness' sake, happy are ye; and be not afraid of their terror, neither be troubled; for it is better, if the will of God be so, that ye suffer for well doing, than for evil doing.   1 PETER 3:14, 17

For ye had compassion of me in my bonds, and took joyfully the spoiling of your goods, knowing in yourselves, that ye have in heaven a better and an enduring substance. Cast not away therefore your confidence, which hath great recompense of reward.

HEBREWS 10:34–35

Beloved, think it not strange concerning the fiery trial which is to try you, as though some strange thing happened unto you; but rejoice, inasmuch as ye are partakers of Christ's suffering; that when his glory shall be revealed, ye may be glad also with exceeding joy. If ye be reproached for the name of Christ, happy are ye; for the Spirit of glory and of God resteth upon you: on their part he is evil spoken of, but on your part he is glorified.

1 PETER 4:12–14

To Them That Are Excommunicated Unjustly

Hear the word of the LORD, ye that tremble at his word: Your brethren that hated you, that cast you out for my name's sake, said, Let the LORD be glorified; but he shall appear to your joy, and they shall be ashamed.

ISAIAH 66:5

Blessed are ye when men shall hate you, and when they shall separate you from their company, and shall reproach you, and cast out your name as evil, for the Son of man's sake. Rejoice ye in that day, and leap for joy: for behold, your reward is great in heaven.

LUKE 6:22–23

3. TO PATIENCE AND SUBMISSION

That ye be not slothful, but followers of them who through faith and patience inherit the promises.

HEBREWS 6:12

It is good that a man should both hope and quietly wait for the salvation of the LORD. It is good for a man that he bear the yoke in his youth. He sitteth alone, and keepeth silence, because he hath borne it upon him. He putteth his mouth in the dust, if so be there may be hope. For the LORD will not cast off for ever.

LAMENTATIONS 3:26–29, 31

The hope of the righteous shall be gladness.

PROVERBS 10:28

We glory in tribulations also: knowing that tribulation worketh patience; and patience, experience; and experience, hope. ROMANS 5:3–4

My brethren, count it all joy, when ye fall into divers temptations; knowing this, that the trying of your faith worketh patience. But let patience have her perfect work, that ye may be perfect and entire, wanting nothing. Blessed is the man that endureth temptation; for when he is tried he shall receive the crown of life, which the Lord hath promised to them that love him. JAMES 1:2–4, 12

Be patient, brethren, unto the coming of the Lord. Behold, the husbandman waiteth for the precious fruit of the earth, and hath long patience for it, until he receive the early and latter rain. Be ye also patient; stablish your hearts: for the coming of the Lord draweth nigh. Behold, we count them happy which endure. Ye have heard of the patience of Job, and have seen the end of the Lord; that the Lord is very pitiful, and of tender mercy.

JAMES 5:7–8, 11

Humble yourselves in the sight of the Lord, and he shall lift you up.   JAMES 4:10

If, when ye do well, and suffer for it, ye take it patiently, this is acceptable with God.   1 PETER 2:20

Humble yourselves therefore under the mighty hand of God, that ye may be exalted in due time.

1 PETER 5:6

Cast not away your confidence, which hath great recompense of reward. For ye have need of patience, that, after ye have done the will of God, ye might receive the promise. For yet a little while, and he that shall come will come, and will not tarry.   HEBREWS 10:35–37

4. TO PERSEVERANCE

Let us not be weary in well doing; for in due season we shall reap, if we faint not.   GALATIANS 6:9

Look to yourselves, that we lose not those things which we have wrought, but that we receive a full reward. Whosoever transgresseth, and abideth not in the doctrine of Christ, hath not God. He that abideth in the doctrine of Christ, he hath both the Father and the Son.

2 JOHN 1:8–9

He that endureth to the end shall be saved.

MATTHEW 10:22; 24:13

Be thou faithful unto death, and I will give thee a crown of life. REVELATION 2:10

If ye continue in my word, then are ye my disciples indeed; and ye shall know the truth, and the truth shall make you free. JOHN 8:31–32

My beloved brethren, be ye steadfast, unmovable, always abounding in the work of the Lord, forasmuch as ye know that your labor is not in vain in the Lord.

1 CORINTHIANS 15:58

Let us hold fast the profession of our faith without wavering; for he is faithful that promised. Cast not away your confidence, which hath great recompense of reward. HEBREWS 10:23, 35

Let that abide in you, which ye have heard from the beginning. If that which ye have heard from the beginning shall remain in you, ye also shall continue in the Son, and in the Father. And now, little children, abide in him; that when he shall appear, we may have confidence, and not be ashamed before him at his coming.

1 JOHN 2:24, 28

If ye abide in me, and my words abide in you, ye shall ask what ye will, and it shall be done unto you.

JOHN 15:7

To Him That Overcomes

Be not overcome of evil, but overcome evil with good.
ROMANS 12:21

He that overcometh shall inherit all things; and I will be his God, and he shall be my son.   REVELATION 21:7

To him that overcometh will I give to eat of the tree of life, which is in the midst of the paradise of God.
REVELATION 2:7

He that overcometh, the same shall be clothed in white raiment; and I will not blot out his name out of the book of life, but I will confess his name before my Father, and before his angels. Him that overcometh will I make a pillar in the temple of my God, and he shall go no more out; and I will write upon him the name of my God, and the name of the city of my God, which is new Jerusalem, which cometh down out of heaven from my God; and I will write upon him my new name. To him that overcometh will I grant to sit with me in my throne, even as I also overcame, and am set down with my Father in his throne.
REVELATION 3:5, 12, 21

He that overcometh shall not be hurt of the second death. To him that overcometh will I give to eat of the hidden manna, and will give him a white stone, and in the stone a new name written, which no man knoweth saving he that receiveth it. And he that overcometh, and keepeth my works unto the end, to him will I give power over the nations. And he shall rule them with a rod of iron; as the vessels of a potter shall they be broken to shivers: even as I received of my Father. And I will give him the morning star.

REVELATION 2:11, 17, 26–28

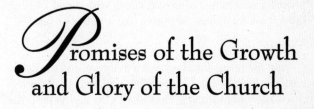

Promises of the Growth
and Glory of the Church

1. THE ENLARGEMENT OF THE CHURCH, AND SPREAD OF THE GOSPEL AND KINGDOM OF CHRIST

Ask of me, and I shall give thee the heathen for thine inheritance, and the uttermost parts of the earth for thy possession. Thou shalt break them with a rod of iron; thou shalt dash them in pieces like a potter's vessel.

PSALM 2:8–9

And the LORD shall be known to Egypt, and the Egyptians shall know the LORD in that day, and shall do sacrifice and oblation; yea, they shall vow a vow unto the LORD, and perform it. In that day shall Israel be the third with Egypt, and with Assyria, even a blessing in the midst of the land; whom the LORD of hosts shall bless, saying, Blessed be Egypt my people, and Assyria the work of my hands, and Israel mine inheritance.

ISAIAH 19:21, 24–25

Princes shall come out of Egypt; Ethiopia shall soon stretch out her hands unto God. PSALM 68:31

That thy way may be known upon earth, thy saving health among all nations. God shall bless us; and all the ends of the earth shall fear him. PSALM 67:2, 7

He shall have dominion from sea to sea, and from the river unto the ends of the earth. Yea, all kings shall fall down before him; all nations shall serve him. His name shall endure for ever; his name shall be continued as long as the sun; and men shall be blessed in him;

all nations shall call him blessed. Let the whole earth be filled with his glory.   PSALM 72:8, 11, 17, 19

And it shall come to pass in the last days, that the mountain of the LORD's house shall be established in the top of the mountains, and shall be exalted above the hills; and all nations shall flow unto it. And many people shall go and say, Come ye, and let us go up to the mountain of the LORD, to the house of the God of Jacob; and he will teach us of his ways, and we will walk in his paths: for out of Zion shall go forth the law, and the word of the LORD from Jerusalem.   ISAIAH 2:2–3; MICAH 4:2

All nations whom thou hast made shall come and worship before thee, O Lord, and shall glorify thy name.
PSALM 86:9

Thy people shall be willing in the day of thy power, in the beauties of holiness from the womb of the morning: thou hast the dew of thy youth.   PSALM 110:3

In that day there shall be a root of Jesse, which shall stand for an ensign of the people; to it shall the Gentiles seek: and his rest shall be glorious.   ISAIAH 11:10

The heathen shall fear the name of the LORD, and all the kings of the earth thy glory. When the LORD shall build up Zion, he shall appear in his glory.
PSALM 102:15–16

All the ends of the world shall remember, and turn unto the LORD; and all the kindreds of the nations shall worship before thee. For the kingdom is the LORD's; and he is the governor among the nations.   PSALM 22:27–28

And her [Tyre's] merchandise and her hire, shall be holiness to the LORD: it shall not be treasured nor laid up: for her merchandise shall be for them that dwell before the LORD, to eat sufficiently, and for durable clothing.
ISAIAH 23:18

He shall cause them that come of Jacob to take root: Israel shall blossom and bud, and fill the face of the world with fruit.   ISAIAH 27:6

The voice of him that crieth in the wilderness, Prepare ye the way of the LORD, make straight in the desert a highway for our God. Every valley shall be exalted, and every mountain and hill shall be made low; and the crooked shall be made straight, and the rough places plain. And the glory of the LORD shall be revealed, and all flesh shall see it together; for the mouth of the Lord hath spoken it.   ISAIAH 40:3–5

Behold my servant, whom I uphold; mine elect, in whom my soul delighteth; I have put my Spirit upon him: he shall bring forth judgment to the Gentiles. He shall not fail nor be discouraged, till he have set judgment in the earth; and the isles shall wait for his law. I the LORD have called thee in righteousness, and will hold thy hand, and will keep thee, and give thee for a covenant of the people, for a light of the Gentiles; to open the blind eyes, to bring out the prisoners from the prison, and them that sit in darkness out of the prisonhouse.   ISAIAH 42:1, 4, 6–7

I have sworn by myself, the word is gone out of my mouth in righteousness, and shall not return, that unto me every knee shall bow, every tongue shall swear. Surely, shall one say, in the LORD have I righteousness and strength: even to him shall men come; and all that are incensed against him shall be ashamed.

ISAIAH 45:23–24; SEE VERSE 14

And he said, It is a light thing that thou shouldest be my servant, to raise up the tribes of Jacob, and to restore the preserved of Israel; I will also give thee for a light to the Gentiles, that thou mayest be my salvation unto the end of the earth. Behold, these shall come from far: and lo, these from the north, and from the west; and these from the land of Sinim. Lift up thine eyes round about, and behold: all these gather themselves together; and come to thee. As I live, saith the LORD, thou shalt surely clothe thee with them all, as with an ornament, and bind them on thee as a bride doeth. The children which thou shalt have, after thou hast lost the other, shall say again in thine ears, The place is too strait for me: give place to me that I may dwell.

ISAIAH 49:6, 12, 18, 20; SEE VERSES 8–9, 11, 19, 21, 22, AND 60:4

The LORD hath made bare his holy arm in the eyes of all the nations; and all the ends of the earth shall see the salvation of our God.   ISAIAH 52:10

The Gentiles shall come to thy light, and kings to the brightness of thy rising. Who are these that fly as a cloud, and as the doves to their windows? Surely the isles shall wait for me, and the ships of Tarshish first, to bring thy sons from far, their silver and their gold with them, unto the name of the LORD thy God, and to the Holy One of Israel, because he hath glorified thee. And the sons of strangers shall build up thy walls, etc.

ISAIAH 60:3, 8–10; SEE VERSES 4–7, 11, 16

Hearken unto me, my people; and give ear unto me, O my nation; for a law shall proceed from me, and I will make my judgment to rest for a light of the people. My righteousness is near; my salvation is gone forth, and mine arms shall judge the people; the isles shall wait upon me, and on mine arm shall they trust. I have put my words in thy mouth, and I have covered thee in the shadow of my hand, that I may plant the heavens, and lay the foundations of the earth, and say unto Zion, Thou art my people. ISAIAH 51:4–5, 16

Behold, I have given him for a witness to the people, a leader and commander to the people. Behold, thou shalt call a nation that thou knowest not, and nations that knew not thee shall run unto thee, because of the LORD thy God, and for the Holy One of Israel; for he hath glorified thee. ISAIAH 55:4–5

So shall they fear the name of the LORD from the west, and his glory from the rising of the sun. When the enemy shall come in like a flood, the Spirit of the LORD shall lift up a standard against him. And the Redeemer shall come to Zion, and unto them that turn from transgression in Jacob, saith the LORD. ISAIAH 59:19–20

Sing, O barren, thou that didst not bear; break forth into singing, and cry aloud, thou that didst not travail with child; for more are the children of the desolate than the children of the married wife, saith the LORD. Enlarge the place of thy tent, and let them stretch forth the curtains of thy habitations; spare not, lengthen thy cords, and strengthen thy stakes; for thou shalt break forth on the right hand and on the left; and thy seed shall inherit the Gentiles, and make the desolate cities to be inhabited.

ISAIAH 54:1–3

This gospel of the kingdom shall be preached in all the world for a witness unto all nations; and then shall the end come.　　　　　　　　MATTHEW 24:14

Who hath heard such a thing? Who hath seen such things? Shall the earth be made to bring forth in one day? or shall a nation be born at once? For as soon as Zion travailed, she brought forth her children. Shall I bring to the birth, and not cause to bring forth? saith the LORD; shall I cause to bring forth, and shut the womb? saith thy God. It shall come, that I will gather all nations and tongues; and they shall come, and see my glory. And I will set a sign among them, and I will send those that escape of them unto the nations, to Tarshish, Pul, and Lud, that draw the bow, to Tubal and Javan, to the isles afar off, that have not heard my fame, neither have seen my glory; and they shall declare my glory among the Gentiles. And they shall bring all your brethren for an offering unto the LORD, out of all nations. And it shall come to pass, that from one new moon to another, and from one Sabbath to another, shall all flesh come to worship before me, saith the LORD.

ISAIAH 66:8–9, 18–20, 23

Sing and rejoice, O daughter of Zion; for lo, I come, and I will dwell in the midst of thee, saith the LORD. And many nations shall be joined to the LORD in that day, and shall be my people; and I will dwell in the midst of thee, and thou shalt know that the LORD of hosts hath sent me unto thee.   ZECHARIAH 2:10–11

And in the days of these kings shall the God of heaven set up a kingdom, which shall never be destroyed: and the kingdom shall not be left to other people, but it shall break in pieces and consume all these kingdoms, and it shall stand for ever.   DANIEL 2:44

I saw in the night visions, and behold, one like the Son of man came with the clouds of heaven, and came to the Ancient of days, and they brought him near before him. And there was given him dominion, and glory, and a kingdom, that all people, nations, and languages, should serve him. And the kingdom, and dominion, and the greatness of the kingdom under the whole heaven, shall be given to the people of the saints of the Most High, whose kingdom is an everlasting kingdom, and all dominions shall serve and obey him.
                    DANIEL 7:13–14, 27

And the LORD shall be king over all the earth; in that day shall there be one LORD, and his name one.
                    ZECHARIAH 14:9

I say unto you, That many shall come from the east and west, and shall sit down with Abraham, and Isaac, and Jacob, in the kingdom of heaven. MATTHEW 8:11

In that day will I raise up the tabernacle of David that is fallen, and close up the breaches thereof; and I will raise up his ruins, and I will build it as in the days of old: that they may possess the remnant of Edom [or, that the residue of men might seek after the Lord, Acts 15:17], and of all the heathen which are called by my name, saith the LORD that doeth this.   AMOS 9:11–12

When thou shalt make his soul an offering for sin, he shall see his seed, he shall prolong his days, and the pleasure of the LORD shall prosper in his hand. He shall see of the travail of his soul, and shall be satisfied: by his knowledge shall my righteous servant justify many; for he shall bear their iniquities. Therefore will I divide him a portion with the great, and he shall divide the spoil with the strong.   ISAIAH 53:10–12

And I, if I be lifted up from the earth, will draw all men unto me.   JOHN 12:32

And they that are far off shall come and build in the temple of the LORD.   ZECHARIAH 6:15

Behold, I create new heavens and a new earth: and the former shall not be remembered, nor come into mind.   ISAIAH 65:17

From the rising of the sun even unto the going down of the same, my name shall be great among the Gentiles; and in every place incense shall be offered unto my name, and a pure offering: for my name shall be great among the heathen, saith the LORD of hosts.
                    MALACHI 1:11

And the inhabitants of one city shall go to another, saying, Let us go speedily to pray before the Lord, and to seek the LORD of hosts: I will go also. Yea, many people and strong nations shall come to seek the LORD of hosts in Jerusalem, and to pray before the LORD. Thus saith the LORD of hosts, In those days it shall come to pass, that ten men shall take hold out of all languages of the nations, even shall take hold of the skirt of him that is a Jew, saying, We will go with you; for we have heard that God is with you.   ZECHARIAH 8:21–23

And the seventh angel sounded, and there were great voices in heaven, saying, The kingdoms of this world are become the kingdoms of our Lord, and of his Christ; and he shall reign for ever and ever.
        REVELATION 11:15; SEE REVELATION 7:9–10; 12:10

2. GLORY OF THE CHURCH

And he carried me away in the spirit to a great and high mountain, and showed me that great city, the holy Jerusalem, descending out of heaven from God, having the glory of God: and her light was like unto a stone most precious, even like a jasper stone, clear as crystal [see verses 18, 21]. And I saw no temple therein, for the Lord God Almighty and the Lamb are the temple of it. And the city had no need of the sun, neither of the moon, to shine in it; for the glory of God did lighten it, and the Lamb is the light thereof. And the nations of them which are saved shall walk in the light of it: and the kings of the earth do bring their glory and honor into it. And the gates of it shall not be shut at all by day; for there shall be no night there. And they shall bring the glory and honor of the nations into it. REVELATION 21:10–11, 22–26

The king's daughter is all glorious within: her clothing is of wrought gold. PSALM 45:13

O thou afflicted, tossed with tempest, and not comforted, behold, I will lay the stones with fair colors, and lay thy foundations with sapphires. And I will make thy windows of agates, and thy gates of carbuncles, and all thy borders of pleasant stones. ISAIAH 54:11–12

Arise, shine; for thy light is come, and the glory of the LORD is risen upon thee. For, behold, the darkness shall cover the earth, and gross darkness the people; but the LORD shall arise upon thee, and his glory shall be seen upon thee. The glory of Lebanon shall come unto thee, the fir tree, the pine tree, and the box together, to beautify the place of my sanctuary; and I will make the place of my feet glorious. Whereas thou hast been forsaken and hated, so that no man went through thee, I will make thee an eternal excellency, a joy of many generations. The sun shall be no more thy light by day; neither for brightness shall the moon give light unto thee: but the LORD shall be unto thee an everlasting light, and thy God thy glory. ISAIAH 60:1–2, 13, 15, 19

Glorious things are spoken of thee, O city of God.
PSALM 87:3

I bring near my righteousness; it shall not be far off, and my salvation shall not tarry; and I will place salvation in Zion for Israel my glory. ISAIAH 46:13

The Gentiles shall see thy righteousness, and all kings thy glory; and thou shalt be called by a new name, which the mouth of the LORD shall name. Thou shalt also be a crown of glory in the hand of the LORD, and a royal diadem in the hand of thy God.　　ISAIAH 62:2–3

Beautiful for situation, the joy of the whole earth, is mount Zion, on the sides of the north, the city of the great King. Walk about Zion, and go round about her: tell the towers thereof. Mark ye well her bulwarks, consider her palaces; that ye may tell it to the generation following.　　PSALM 48:2, 12–13

3. INCREASE OF LIGHT AND KNOWLEDGE, AND THE MEANS OF GRACE

And all thy children shall be taught of the LORD.
ISAIAH 54:13

Many shall run to and fro, and knowledge shall be increased.　　DANIEL 12:4

The earth shall be full of the knowledge of the LORD, as the waters cover the sea.　　ISAIAH 11:9

And in this mountain shall the LORD of hosts make unto all people a feast of fat things, a feast of wines on the lees, of fat things full of marrow, of wines on the lees well refined. And he will destroy in this mountain the face of the covering cast over all people, and the veil that is spread over all nations.　　ISAIAH 25:6–7

I will open rivers in high places, and fountains in the midst of the valleys: I will make the wilderness a pool of water, and the dry land springs of water. I will plant in the wilderness the cedar, the shittah tree, and the myrtle, and the oil tree. I will set in the desert the fir tree, and the pine, and the box tree together.

ISAIAH 41:18–19; SEE ISAIAH 35:6–8

How beautiful upon the mountains are the feet of him that bringeth good tidings, that publisheth peace; that bringeth good tidings of good, that publisheth salvation; that saith unto Zion, Thy God reigneth! Thy watchmen shall lift up the voice; with the voice together shall they sing; for they shall see eye to eye, when the LORD shall bring again Zion.   ISAIAH 52:7–8

In that day shall the deaf hear the words of the book, and the eyes of the blind shall see out of obscurity, and out of darkness. They also that erred in spirit shall come to understanding, and they that murmured shall learn doctrine.   ISAIAH 29:18, 24

4. INCREASE OF PURITY, HOLINESS, AND RIGHTEOUSNESS

The LORD is exalted; for he dwelleth on high: he hath filled Zion with judgment and righteousness. And wisdom and knowledge shall be the stability of thy times, and strength of salvation: the fear of the LORD is his treasure.

ISAIAH 33:5–6

Thy people shall be all righteous; they shall inherit the land for ever, the branch of my planting, the work of my hands, that I may be glorified.   ISAIAH 60:21

And it shall come to pass, that he that is left in Zion, and he that remaineth in Jerusalem, shall be called holy, even every one that is written among the living in Jerusalem; when the LORD shall have washed away the filth of the daughters of Zion, and shall have purged the blood of Jerusalem from the midst thereof, by the spirit of judgment, and by the spirit of burning.   ISAIAH 4:3–4

And to her [the Lamb's wife] was granted that she should be arrayed in fine linen, clean, and white; for the fine linen is the righteousness of saints.   REVELATION 19:8

Until the Spirit be poured upon us from on high, and the wilderness be a fruitful field, and the fruitful field be counted for a forest. Then judgment shall dwell in the wilderness, and righteousness remain in the fruitful field.
     ISAIAH 32:15–16

He shall sit as a refiner and purifier of silver; and he shall purify the sons of Levi, and purge them as gold and silver, that they may offer unto the Lord an offering in righteousness. Then shall the offering of Judah and Jerusalem be pleasant unto the Lord, as in the days of old, and as in former years.   MALACHI 3:3–4

In that day shall there be upon the bells of the horses, HOLINESS UNTO THE LORD; and the pots in the LORD's house shall be like the bowls before the altar. Yea, every pot in Jerusalem and in Judah shall be holiness unto the LORD of hosts; and all they that sacrifice shall come and take of them, and seethe therein: and in that day there shall be no more the Canaanite in the house of the LORD of hosts.   ZECHARIAH 14:20–21

They shall fear thee as long as the sun and moon endure, throughout all generations.   PSALM 72:5

Drop down, ye heavens, from above, and let the skies pour down righteousness: let the earth open, and let them bring forth salvation, and let righteousness spring up together; I the LORD have created it.   ISAIAH 45:8

As the earth bringeth forth her bud, and as the garden causeth the things that are sown in it to spring forth; so the Lord GOD will cause righteousness and praise to spring forth before all the nations.   ISAIAH 61:11

Mercy and truth are met together; righteousness and peace have kissed each other. Truth shall spring out of the earth, and righteousness shall look down from heaven. Righteousness shall go before him, and shall set us in the way of his steps.   PSALM 85:10–11, 13

5. PEACE, LOVE, AND UNITY

And they shall beat their swords into plowshares, and their spears into pruninghooks: nation shall not lift up sword against nation, neither shall they learn war any more.   ISAIAH 2:4

Neither pray I for these alone, but for them also which shall believe on me through their word; that they all may be one, as thou, Father, art in me, and I in thee, that they also may be one in us: that the world may believe thou hast sent me. And the glory which thou gavest me, I have given them; that they may be one, even as we are one: I in them, and thou in me, that they may be made perfect in one; and that the world may know thou hast sent me, and hast loved them as thou hast loved me.

JOHN 17:20–23

The wolf also shall dwell with the lamb, and the leopard shall lie down with the kid; and the calf, and the young lion, and the fatling together; and a little child shall lead them. And the cow and the bear shall feed; their young ones shall lie down together: and the lion shall eat straw like the ox. And the sucking child shall play on the hole of the asp, and the weaned child shall put his hand on the cockatrice's den. They shall not hurt nor destroy in all my holy mountain. The envy also of Ephraim shall depart, and the adversaries of Judah shall be cut off; Ephraim shall not envy Judah, and Judah shall not vex Ephraim.

ISAIAH 11:6–9, 13

The mountains shall bring peace to the people, and the little hills, by righteousness. In his days shall the righteous flourish; and abundance of peace so long as the moon endureth.   PSALM 72:3, 7

From whom [Christ] the whole body fitly joined together and compacted by that which every joint supplieth, according to the effectual working in the measure of every part, maketh increase of the body unto the edifying of itself in love.   EPHESIANS 4:16

6. SUBMISSION AND DESTRUCTION OF THE ENEMIES OF THE CHURCH

In the day the LORD with his sore and great and strong sword shall punish leviathan the piercing serpent, even leviathan that crooked serpent; and he shall slay the dragon that is in the sea.   ISAIAH 27:1

The LORD shall send the rod of thy strength out of Zion: rule thou in the midst of thine enemies. The Lord at thy right hand shall strike through kings in the day of his wrath. He shall judge among the heathen, he shall fill the places with the dead bodies; he shall wound the heads over many countries.   PSALM 110:2, 5–6

When the enemy shall come in like a flood, the Spirit of the LORD shall lift up a standard against him.
                                        ISAIAH 59:19

He shall smite the earth with the rod of his mouth, and with the breath of his lips shall he slay the wicked.
                                        ISAIAH 11:4

Behold, all they that were incensed against thee shall be ashamed and confounded: they shall be as nothing: and they that strive with thee shall perish. Thou shalt seek them, and shalt not find them, even them that contended with thee: they that war against thee shall be as nothing, and as a thing of naught.
                    ISAIAH 41:11–12; SEE VERSES 15–16

Shall the prey be taken from the mighty, or the lawful captive delivered? But thus saith the LORD, Even the captives of the mighty shall be taken away, and the prey of the terrible shall be delivered; for I will contend with him that contendeth with thee, and I will save thy children. And I will feed them that oppress thee with their own flesh; and they shall be drunken with their own blood, as with sweet wine; and all flesh shall know that I the LORD am thy Saviour and thy Redeemer, the mighty one of Jacob. ISAIAH 49:24–26

The sons also of them that afflicted thee shall come bending unto thee; and all they that despised thee shall bow themselves down at the soles of thy feet; and they shall call thee, The city of the LORD, The Zion of the Holy One of Israel. ISAIAH 60:14

The Destruction of Antichrist, Babylon, Etc.

Then shall that Wicked be revealed, whom the Lord shall consume with the spirit of his mouth, and shall destroy with the brightness of his coming.
2 THESSALONIANS 2:8; SEE DANIEL 7:24–26

If any man worship the beast and his image, and receive his mark in his forehead, or in his hand, the same shall drink of the wine of the wrath of God, which is poured out without mixture into the cup of his indignation.
REVELATION 14:9–10

For thus saith the Lord GOD; When I shall make thee a desolate city, like cities that are not inhabited; when I shall bring up the deep upon thee, and great waters shall cover thee; I will make thee a terror, thou shalt be no more: though thou be sought for, yet shalt thou never be found again, saith the Lord GOD.

EZEKIEL 26:19, 21

Babylon the great is fallen, is fallen, and is become the habitation of devils, and the hold of every foul spirit, and the cage of every unclean and hateful bird.

REVELATION 18:2; SEE TO THE END OF THE CHAPTER

And I saw the beast, and the kings of the earth, and their armies, gathered together to make war against Him that sat on the horse, and against his army. And the beast was taken, and with him the false prophet that wrought miracles before him, with which he deceived them that had received the mark of the beast, and them that worshipped his image. These both were cast alive into a lake of fire burning with brimstone. REVELATION 19:19–20

And when the thousand years are expired, Satan shall be loosed out of his prison; and shall go out to deceive the nations which are in the four quarters of the earth, Gog and Magog, to gather them together to battle; the number of whom is as the sand of the sea. And they went up on the breadth of the earth, and compassed the camp of the saints about, and the beloved city; and fire came down from God out of heaven and devoured them.

REVELATION 20:7–9; SEE EZEKIEL 38–39

7. FAVOR AND SUBMISSION OF KINGS TO THE KINGDOM OF CHRIST

So shall he sprinkle many nations; the kings shall shut their mouths at him: for that which had not been told them shall they see; and that which they had not heard shall they consider.   Isaiah 52:15

Thus saith the Lord, the Redeemer of Israel, and his Holy One, to him whom man despiseth, to him whom the nation abhorreth, to a servant of rulers, Kings shall see and arise, princes also shall worship, because of the Lord that is faithful, and the Holy One of Israel, and he shall choose thee. And kings shall be thy nursing fathers, and their queens thy nursing mothers: they shall bow down to thee with their face toward the earth, and lick up the dust of thy feet; and thou shalt know that I am the Lord; for they shall not be ashamed that wait for me.   Isaiah 49:7, 23

And the Gentiles shall come to thy light, and kings to the brightness of thy rising. And the sons of strangers shall build up thy walls, and their kings shall minister unto thee; for in my wrath I smote thee, but in my favor have I had mercy on thee. Therefore thy gates shall be open continually; they shall not be shut day nor night; that men may bring unto thee the forces of the Gentiles, and that their kings may be brought. Thou shalt suck the milk of the Gentiles, and shalt suck the breast of kings; and thou shalt know that I the Lord am thy Saviour and thy Redeemer, the Mighty One of Jacob.
        Isaiah 60:3, 10–11, 16

8. THE SECURITY, TRANQUILLITY, AND PROSPERITY OF THE CHURCH

The LORD shall comfort Zion: he will comfort all her waste places; and he will make her wilderness like Eden, and her desert like the garden of the LORD; joy and gladness shall be found therein, thanksgiving, and the voice of melody.　　　　　　　　　　　　　ISAIAH 51:3

Look upon Zion, the city of our solemnities; thine eyes shall see Jerusalem a quiet habitation, a tabernacle that shall not be taken down; not one of the stakes thereof shall ever be removed, neither shall any of the cords thereof be broken. But there the glorious LORD will be unto us a place of broad rivers and streams, wherein shall go no galley with oars, neither shall gallant ship pass thereby. For the LORD is our judge, the LORD is our lawgiver, the LORD is our king; he will save us.
　　　　　　　　　　　　　ISAIAH 33:20–22

Upon this rock I will build my church, and the gates of hell shall not prevail against it.　　　MATTHEW 16:18

In righteousness shalt thou be established: thou shalt be far from oppression; for thou shalt not fear: and from terror; for it shall not come near thee. Behold, they shall surely gather together, but not by me: whosoever shall gather together against thee shall fall for thy sake. No weapon that is formed against thee shall prosper; and every tongue that shall rise against thee in judgment thou shalt condemn. This is the heritage of the servants of the LORD, and their righteousness is of me, saith the LORD.
　　　　　　　　　　　　　ISAIAH 54:14–15, 17

Rejoice ye with Jerusalem, and be glad with her, all ye that love her: rejoice for joy with her, all ye that mourn for her; that ye may suck, and be satisfied with the breasts of her consolations; that ye may milk out, and be delighted with the abundance of her glory. For thus saith the LORD, Behold, I will extend peace to her like a river, and the glory of the Gentiles like a flowing stream; then shall ye suck, ye shall be borne upon her sides, and be dandled upon her knees.

ISAIAH 66:10–12; SEE VERSES 13–14

In his days shall Judah be saved, and Jerusalem shall dwell safely.   JEREMIAH 33:16

In that day sing ye unto her, A vineyard of red wine. I the LORD do keep it; I will water it every moment; lest any hurt it, I will keep it night and day.

ISAIAH 27:2–3

And the kingdom and dominion, and the greatness of the kingdom under the whole heaven, shall be given to the people of the saints of the Most High, whose kingdom is an everlasting kingdom, and all dominions shall serve and obey him.   DANIEL 7:27

Thou shalt arise, and have mercy upon Zion; for the time to favor her, yea, the set time, is come. For thy servants take pleasure in her stones, and favor the dust thereof. When the LORD shall build up Zion, he shall appear in his glory.   PSALM 102:13–14, 16

And the LORD will create upon every dwellingplace of mount Zion, and upon her assemblies, a cloud and smoke by day, and the shining of a flaming fire by night; for upon all the glory shall be a defence. And there shall be a tabernacle for a shadow in the daytime from the heat, and for a place of refuge, and for a covert from storm and from rain.   ISAIAH 4:5–6

Be ye glad and rejoice for ever in that which I create; for, behold, I create Jerusalem a rejoicing, and her people a joy. And I will rejoice in Jerusalem, and joy in my people; and the voice of weeping shall be no more heard in her, nor the voice of crying.   ISAIAH 65:18–19

9. THE PERPETUAL CONTINUANCE OF THE CHURCH

For as the new heavens and the new earth which I will make, shall remain before me, saith the LORD, so shall your seed and your name remain.   ISAIAH 66:22

Thus saith the LORD, which giveth the sun for a light by day, and the ordinances of the moon and of the stars for a light by night, which divideth the sea when the waves thereof roar; The LORD of hosts is his name: If those ordinances depart from before me, saith the LORD, then the seed of Israel also shall cease from being a nation before me for ever. Thus saith the LORD: If heaven above can be measured, and the foundations of the earth searched out beneath, I will also cast off all the seed of Israel, for all that they have done, saith the LORD.
JEREMIAH 31:35–37; 33:20–22, 25–26

Lo, I am with you always, even unto the end of the world. MATTHEW 28:20

He shall reign over the house of Jacob for ever; and of his kingdom there shall be no end. LUKE 1:33

His dominion is an everlasting dominion, which shall not pass away, and his kingdom that which shall not be destroyed. DANIEL 7:14

The kingdoms of this world are become the kingdoms of our Lord, and of his Christ; and he shall reign for ever and ever. REVELATION 11:15

In the days of these kings shall the God of heaven set up a kingdom, which shall never be destroyed: and the kingdom shall not be left to other people, but it shall break in pieces and consume all these kingdoms, and it shall stand for ever. DANIEL 2:44

As for me, this is my covenant with them, saith the LORD: My Spirit that is upon thee, and my words which I have put in thy mouth, shall not depart out of thy mouth, nor out of the mouth of thy seed, nor out of the mouth of thy seed's seed, saith the LORD, from henceforth and for ever. ISAIAH 59:21

10. THE CONVERSION AND RESTORATION
OF THE JEWS

And men shall dwell in it [that is, all the land], and there shall be no more utter destruction; but Jerusalem shall be safely inhabited.
ZECHARIAH 14:11; SEE THE WHOLE CHAPTER

Nevertheless, I will remember my covenant with thee in the days of thy youth, and I will establish unto thee an everlasting covenant. Thou shalt remember thy ways, and be ashamed, when thou shalt receive thy sisters, thine elder and thy younger [Sodom and Samaria, v. 55]: and I will give them unto thee for daughters, but not by thy covenant.　　EZEKIEL 16:60-61; SEE ALSO VERSES 62-63

Yet the number of the children of Israel shall be as the sand of the sea, which cannot be measured nor numbered; and it shall come to pass, that in the place where it was said unto them, Ye are not my people, there it shall be said unto them, Ye are the sons of the living God. Then shall the children of Judah and the children of Israel be gathered together, and appoint themselves one head, and they shall come up out of the land; for great shall be the day of Jezreel.　　HOSEA 1:10-11

And I will cause the captivity of Judah and the captivity of Israel to return, and will build them, as at the first. And I will cleanse them from all their iniquity, etc. And it shall be to me a name of joy, a praise and an honor before all the nations of the earth, which shall hear all the good that I do unto them, etc. In those days, and at that time, will I cause the Branch of righteousness to grow up unto David; and he shall execute judgment and righteousness in the land. In those days shall Judah be saved, and Jerusalem shall dwell safely: and this is the name wherewith she shall be called, The LORD our righteousness. Considerest thou not what this people have spoken, saying, The two families which the LORD hath chosen he hath even cast them off, etc. Thus saith the LORD: If my covenant be not with day and night, and if I have not appointed the ordinances of heaven and earth; then will I cast away the seed of Jacob, and David my servant, so that I will not take any of his seed to be rulers over the seed of Abraham, Isaac, and Jacob; for I will cause their captivity to return, and have mercy on them.

JEREMIAH 33:7–9, 15–16, 24–26; TO THE SAME PUR-
POSE SEE THE WHOLE CHAPTER; SEE ALSO CHAPTER
50:4–5, 19–20

I will surely assemble, O Jacob, all of thee: I will surely father the remnant of Israel; I will put them together as the sheep of Bozrah, as the flock in the midst of their fold; they shall make great noise, by reason of the multitude of men. The breaker is come up before them: they have broken up, and have passed through the gate, and are gone out by it; and their king shall pass before them, and the LORD on the head of them.

MICAH 2:12–13

I will multiply upon you [the mountains of Israel] man and beast; and they shall increase, and bring fruit: and I will settle you after your old estates, and will do better unto you than at your beginnings; and ye shall know that I am the LORD. I will take you from among the heathen, and gather you out of all countries, and will bring you into your own land. Then will I sprinkle clean water upon you, and ye shall be clean; from all your filthiness, and from all your idols, will I cleanse you. A new heart also will I give you, etc. In the day that I shall have cleansed you from all your iniquities I will also cause you to dwell in the cities, and the wastes shall be builded.

EZEKIEL 36:11, 24–26, 33; SEE THE WHOLE CHAPTER, ALSO CHAPTER 37

Jerusalem shall be trodden down of the Gentiles, until the times of the Gentiles be fulfilled.   LUKE 21:24

And they shall dwell in the land that I have given unto Jacob my servant, wherein your fathers have dwelt; and they shall dwell therein, even they, and their children, and their children's children for ever: and my servant David shall be their prince for ever.

EZEKIEL 37:25

I will bring you out from the people, and will gather you out of the countries wherein ye are scattered, with a mighty hand. And I will bring you into the wilderness of the people, and there will I plead with you face to face. And I will cause you to pass under the rod, and I will bring you into the bond of the covenant: and I will purge out from among you the rebels, and them that transgress against me. In my holy mountain, in the mountain of the height of Israel, saith the Lord GOD, there shall all the house of Israel, all of them in the land, serve me: there will I accept them, and there will I require your offerings, and the firstfruits of your oblations, with all your holy things.

EZEKIEL 20:34–35, 37–38, 40; SEE ALSO VERSES 41, 44

Yea, I will rejoice over them to do them good, and I will plant them in this land assuredly with my whole heart, and with my whole soul.

JEREMIAH 32:41; SEE FROM VERSE 37 TO THE END

And I will set up one shepherd over them, and he shall feed them, even my servant David; he shall feed them, and he shall be their shepherd. And I the Lord will be their God, and my servant David a prince among them; I the Lord have spoken it. And they shall no more be a prey to the heathen, neither shall the beasts of the land devour them; but they shall dwell safely, and none shall make them afraid. And I will raise up for them a plant of renown.

EZEKIEL 34:23–24, 28–29; SEE ALSO VERSES 11, 16,
AND FROM VERSE 22 TO THE END OF THE CHAPTER

Behold, I will allure her, and bring her into the wilderness, and speak comfortably unto her. I will give her her vineyards from thence, and the valley of Achor for a door of hope; and she shall sing there, as in the days of her youth, and as in the day when she came up out of the land of Egypt. And I will betroth thee unto me for ever, etc.

HOSEA 2:14–15, 19; SEE FROM VERSE 16 TO THE END

Even unto this day, when Moses is read, the veil is upon their heart. Nevertheless, when it shall turn to the Lord, the veil shall be taken away.

2 CORINTHIANS 3:15–16

Sing and rejoice, O daughter of Zion; for lo, I come, and I will dwell in the midst of thee, saith the Lord. And the LORD shall inherit Judah his portion in the holy land, and shall choose Jerusalem again.

ZECHARIAH 2:10, 12

Therefore will he give them up, until the time that she which travaileth hath brought forth: then the remnant of his brethren shall return unto the children of Israel. And he shall stand and feed in the strength of the LORD his God; and they shall abide: for now shall he be great unto the ends of the earth. And the remnant of Jacob shall be in the midst of many people, as a dew from the LORD, as the showers upon the grass, that tarrieth not for man, nor waiteth for the sons of men. Thy graven images also will I cut off, and thy standing images out of the midst of thee; and thou shalt no more worship the work of thy hands.

MICAH 5:3–4, 7, 13; SEE THE WHOLE CHAPTER, CHAPTER 4, AND CHAPTER 7:14, 17; SEE ALSO ZEPHANIAH 3:9, TO THE END

Upon mount Zion shall be deliverance, and there shall be holiness; and the house of Jacob shall possess their possessions. And saviours shall come up on mount Zion to judge the mount of Esau; and the kingdom shall be the LORD's.   OBADIAH 1:17, 21

The children of Israel shall abide many days without a king, and without a prince, and without a sacrifice, and without an image, and without an ephod, and without teraphim. Afterward shall the children of Israel return, and seek the LORD their God, and David their king; and shall fear the LORD and his goodness in the latter days.

HOSEA 3:4–5

Behold, in those days, and in that time, when I shall bring again the captivity of Judah and Jerusalem, I will also gather all nations, and will bring them down into the valley of Jehoshaphat, and will plead with them for my people, etc. So shall ye know that I am the LORD your God, dwelling in Zion, my holy mountain: then shall Jerusalem be hold, and there shall no strangers pass through her any more. Judah shall dwell for ever, and Jerusalem from generation to generation.

JOEL 3:1–2, 17, 20; SEE ALSO VERSES 7, 14, 16, 18, 21

And I will strengthen the house of Judah, and I will save the house of Joseph, and I will bring them again to place them; for I have mercy upon them: and they shall be as though I had not cast them off; for I am the LORD their God, and will hear them. I will hiss for them, and gather them; for I have redeemed them: and they shall increase, as they have increased. And I will sow them among the people: and they shall remember me in far countries; and they shall live with their children, and turn again.

ZECHARIAH 10:6, 8–9; SEE THE WHOLE CHAPTER

God hath not cast away his people which he foreknew. If the fall of them be the riches of the world, and the diminishing of them the riches of the Gentiles; how much more their fulness? For if the casting away of them be the reconciling of the world, what shall the receiving of them be, for life from the dead? And they also, if they abide not still in unbelief, shall be grafted in; for God is able to graft them in again. How much more shall these, which be the natural branches, be grafted into their own olive tree? For I would not, brethren, that ye should be ignorant of this mystery lest ye should be wise in your own conceits, that blindness in part is happened to Israel, until the fulness of the Gentiles be come in. And so all Israel shall be saved; as it is written, There shall come out of Zion the Deliverer, and shall turn away ungodliness from Jacob: for this is my covenant unto them, when I shall take away their sins. As concerning the gospel, they are enemies for your sakes; but as touching the election, they are beloved for the Father's sake. For the gifts and calling of God are without repentance. [See also verses 30–32.] God hath concluded them all in unbelief, that he might have mercy upon all. O the depth of the riches both of the wisdom and knowledge of God! How unsearchable are his judgments, and his ways past finding out!

ROMANS 11:2, 12, 15, 23–33

At the same time, saith the LORD, will I be the God of all the families of Israel, and they shall be my people. Again I will build thee, and thou shalt be built, O virgin of Israel: thou shalt again be adorned with thy tabrets, and shalt go forth in the dances of them that make merry. Hear the word of the Lord, O ye nations, and declare it in the isles afar off, and say, He that scattered Israel will gather him, and keep him, as a shepherd doth his flock. There is hope in thine end, that thy children shall come again to their own border. Behold, the days come, saith the LORD, that I will make a new covenant with the house of Israel, and with the house of Judah: not according to the covenant that I made with their fathers, etc. But this shall be the covenant that I will make with the house of Israel after those days, saith the LORD: I will put my law in their inward parts, and write it in their hearts; and will be their God, and they shall be my people. Behold, the days come, saith the Lord, that the city shall be built to the LORD, from the tower of Hananeel unto the gate of the corner.

JEREMIAH 31:1, 4, 10, 17, 31–33, 38; SEE THE WHOLE CHAPTER

In that day will I make the governors of Judah like a hearth of fire among the wood, and like a torch of fire in a sheaf; and they shall devour all the people round about, on the right hand and on the left; and Jerusalem shall be inhabited again, in her own place, even in Jerusalem. And I will pour upon the house of David, and upon the inhabitants of Jerusalem, the spirit of grace and of supplications; and they shall look upon me, whom they have pierced, etc.

ZECHARIAH 12:6, 10; SEE THE WHOLE CHAPTER

And I will bring again the captivity of my people of Israel, and they shall build the waste cities, and inhabit them. And I will plant them upon their land, and they shall be no more pulled up out of their land which I have given them, saith the LORD thy God.   AMOS 9:14–15

They shall serve the LORD their God, and David their king, whom I will raise up unto them. Therefore fear thou not, O my servant Jacob, saith the LORD; neither be dismayed, O Israel; for, lo, I will save thee from afar, and thy seed from the land of their captivity; and Jacob shall return, and shall be in rest, and be quiet, and none shall make him afraid.

JEREMIAH 30:9–10; SEE TO THE END OF THE CHAPTER

Promises of Christ's Second Coming

One

That Christ Will Come Again

Judge nothing before the time, until the Lord come, who both will bring to light the hidden things of darkness, and will make manifest the counsels of the heart.

1 CORINTHIANS 4:5

Henceforth there is laid up for me a crown of righteousness, which the Lord, the righteous Judge, shall give me at that day: and not to me only, but unto all them also that love his appearing.

2 TIMOTHY 4:8

The Lord himself shall descend from heaven with a shout, with the voice of the archangel, and with the trump of God; and the dead in Christ shall rise first; then we which are alive and remain shall be caught up together with them in the clouds, to meet the Lord in the air: and so shall we ever be with the Lord.

1 THESSALONIANS 4:16–17

Watch therefore: for ye know not what hour your Lord doth come. MATTHEW 24:42

Ye have heard how I said unto you, I go away, and come again unto you. JOHN 14:28

To wait for his Son from heaven, whom he raised from the dead, even Jesus. 1 THESSALONIANS 1:10

They shall look upon me whom they have pierced, and they shall mourn for him. ZECHARIAH 12:10

When Christ, who is our life, shall appear, then shall ye also appear with him in glory. COLOSSIANS 3:4

I know that my Redeemer liveth, and that he shall stand at the latter day upon the earth. JOB 19:25

And his feet shall stand in that day upon the Mount of Olives, which is before Jerusalem. ZECHARIAH 14:4

As often as ye eat this bread, and drink this cup, ye do show the Lord's death till he come.
1 CORINTHIANS 11:26

The Lord direct your hearts into the love of God, and into the patient waiting for Christ.
2 THESSALONIANS 3:5

They shall see the Son of man coming in the clouds of heaven with power and great glory.
MATTHEW 24:30

We know that, when he shall appear, we shall be like him; for we shall see him as he is.   1 JOHN 3:2

When the Chief Shepherd shall appear, ye shall receive a crown of glory that fadeth not away.

1 PETER 5:4

Behold, he cometh with clouds; and every eye shall see him, and they also which pierced him.

REVELATION 1:7

Ye shall see the Son of man sitting on the right hand of power, and coming in the clouds of heaven.

MARK 14:62

To you who are troubled rest with us, when the Lord Jesus shall be revealed from heaven with his mighty angels.   2 THESSALONIANS 1:7

If I go and prepare a place for you, I will come again, and receive you unto myself; that where I am, there ye may be also.   JOHN 14:3

As the lightning cometh out of the East, and shineth even unto the West; so shall also the coming of the Son of man be.   MATTHEW 24:27

Looking for that blessed hope, and the glorious appearing of the great God and our Saviour Jesus Christ

TITUS 2:13

This same Jesus, which is taken up from you into heaven, shall so come in like manner as ye have seen him go into heaven.   ACTS 1:11

The Son of man shall come in the glory of his Father with his angels; and then he shall reward every man according to his works.   MATTHEW 16:27

When the Son of man shall come in his glory, and all the holy angels with him, then shall he sit upon the throne of his glory.   MATTHEW 25:31

He shall send Jesus Christ, who before was preached unto you; whom the heaven must receive until the times of restitution of all things.   ACTS 3:20–21

So Christ was once offered to bear the sins of many; and unto them that look for him shall he appear the second time without sin unto salvation.   HEBREWS 9:28

Behold, I come quickly; and my reward is with me, to give every man according as his work shall be. . . . Amen. Even so, come, Lord Jesus.

REVELATION 22:12, 20

To the end he may stablish your hearts unblamable in holiness before God, even our Father, at the coming of our Lord Jesus with all his saints.

1 THESSALONIANS 3:13

Waiting for the coming of our Lord Jesus Christ, who shall also confirm you unto the end, that ye may be blameless in the day of our Lord.   1 CORINTHIANS 1:7–8

I saw in the night visions, and, behold, one like the Son of man came with the clouds of heaven, . . . and there was given him dominion, and glory, and a kingdom, . . . which shall not be destroyed.

DANIEL 7:13–14

Our conversation is in heaven; from whence also we look for the Saviour, the Lord Jesus Christ; who shall change our vile body, . . . according to the working whereby he is able even to subdue all things unto himself.

PHILIPPIANS 3:20–21

There shall come in the last days scoffers, walking after their own lusts, and saying, Where is the promise of his coming? for since the fathers fell asleep, all things continue as they were from the beginning of the creation. . . . But the day of the Lord will come as a thief in the night.

2 PETER 3:3–4, 10

Conclusion

One

That God Will Perform All His Promises

Know, that the LORD thy God, he is God, the faithful God, which keepeth covenant and mercy with them that love him and keep his commandments, to a thousand generations.   DEUTERONOMY 7:9

For ever, O LORD, thy word is settled in heaven. Thy faithfulness is unto all generations. Thy word is true from the beginning.   PSALM 119:89–90, 160

God is not a man, that he should lie; neither the son of man, that he should repent. Hath he said, and shall he not do it? Or hath he spoken, and shall he not make it good?   NUMBERS 23:19

That by two immutable things, in which it was impossible for God to lie, we might have a strong consolation,

143

who have fled by refuge to lay hold upon the hope set before us.   HEBREWS 6:18

The word of the LORD is tried.   PSALM 18:30

He is faithful that promised.   HEBREWS 10:23

Thy counsels of old are faithfulness and truth.
                                                  ISAIAH 25:1

My covenant will I not break, nor alter the thing that is gone out of my lips.   PSALM 89:34

I have spoken it, I will also bring it to pass; I have purposed it, I will also do it.   ISAIAH 46:11

He hath remembered his covenant for ever, the word which he commanded to a thousand generations.
                                                  PSALM 105:8

Ye know in all your hearts and in all your souls, that not one thing hath failed of all the good things which the LORD your God spake concerning you; all are come to pass unto you, and not one thing hath failed thereof.
                                   JOSHUA 23:14; 1 KINGS 8:56

The mountains shall depart, and the hills be removed; but my kindness shall not depart from thee, neither shall the covenant of my peace be removed, saith the LORD that hath mercy on thee.   ISAIAH 54:10

If we believe not, yet he abideth faithful; he cannot deny himself.   2 TIMOTHY 2:13

The Lord is not slack concerning his promise, as some men count slackness.   2 PETER 3:9

Being fully persuaded that, what he had promised, he was able also to perform.   ROMANS 4:21

All the promises of God in him are yea, and in him Amen, unto the glory of God.   2 CORINTHIANS 1:20

In hope of eternal life, which God, that cannot lie, promised before the world began.   TITUS 1:2

The strength of Israel will not lie nor repent: for he is not a man, that he should repent.   1 SAMUEL 15:29

He will not forsake thee, . . . nor forget the covenant of thy fathers which he sware unto them.
                                        DEUTERONOMY 4:31

They that know thy name will put their trust in thee; for thou, LORD, hast not forsaken them that seek thee.
                                        PSALM 9:10

Whereby are given unto us exceeding great and precious promises.   2 PETER 1:4

Helpful Thoughts
for Special
Occasions

One

For a Birthday

The Lord thy God is with thee whithersoever thou goest.   Joshua 1:9

Oh, how great is thy goodness which thou hast laid up for them that fear thee! . . . Thou shalt hide them in the secret of thy presence from the pride of man; thou shalt keep them secretly in a pavilion from the strife of tongues.–He that dwelleth in the secret place of the Most High shall abide under the shadow of the Almighty.

Every place that the sole of your foot shall tread upon, that have I given unto you . . . As I was with Moses, so I will be with thee: I will not fail thee nor forsake thee.– The land whither ye go to possess it is a land of hills and valleys. . . . A land which the Lord thy God careth for: the eyes of the Lord thy God are always upon it, from the beginning of the year even unto the end of the year.– Ye are God's husbandry.–Created in Christ Jesus unto good works, which God hath before ordained that we should walk in them.

JOSHUA 1:3, 5; DEUTERONOMY 11:11–12; 1 CORINTHIANS 3:9; EPHESIANS 2:10; PSALM 31:19–20; PSALM 91:1

Two

The New Home

I will walk within my house with a perfect heart.

PSALM 101:2

As for me and my house, we will serve the LORD.

Our sufficiency is of God.–I the LORD thy God will hold thy right hand, saying unto thee, Fear not; I will help thee.

Seek ye first the kingdom of God and his righteousness, and all these things shall be added unto you.– No servant can serve two masters: ye cannot serve God and mammon.

Husbands, love your wives.–That the young women love their husbands.–Not easily provoked.–Be ye kind one to another, tenderhearted, forgiving one another, even as God for Christ's sake hath forgiven you.

Being heirs together of the grace of life.—Two are better than one; for if they fall, the one will lift up his fellow.—Let us consider one another to provoke unto love and to good works.

Joshua 24:15; Matthew 6:33; Luke 16:13; 1 Peter 3:7; Ecclesiastes 4:9–10; Hebrews 10:24; Colossians 3:19; Titus 2:4; 1 Corinthians 13:5; Ephesians 4:32; 2 Corinthians 3:5; Isaiah 41:13

Three

For Sickness

Have mercy upon me, O LORD, for I am weak. O
LORD, heal me.   PSALM 6:2

Now our Lord Jesus Christ himself, and God, even
our Father, which hath loved us and hath given us everlasting consolation and good hope through grace, comfort your hearts.

Be not far from me, for trouble is near.–Thou art near,
O LORD.–Thou hast heard my voice. Thou drewest near
in the day that I called upon thee: thou saidest, Fear not.–
A very present help.

When my heart is overwhelmed, lead me to the Rock
that is higher than I.–He giveth power to the faint, and
to them that have no might he increaseth strength.–The
LORD is the strength of my life.

O LORD, I am oppressed; undertake for me.—A bruised reed shall he not break.—Yea, though I walk through the valley of the shadow of death I will fear no evil, for thou art with me.—Underneath are the everlasting arms.

PSALM 61:2; ISAIAH 40:29; PSALM 27:1; PSALM 22:11; PSALM 119:151; LAMENTATIONS 3:56–57; ISAIAH 46:1; ISAIAH 38:14; MATTHEW 12:20; PSALM 23:4; DEUTERONOMY 33:27; 2 THESSALONIANS 2:16–17

Four

Times of Anxiety

Fear not: I will help thee.   ISAIAH 41:13

Fear not; I am the first and the last.

Come unto me, all ye that labor and are heavy laden, and I will give you rest.—All the promises of God in him are Yea, and in him. Amen.

He shall call upon me, and I will answer him: I will be with him in trouble.—I have made and I will bear; even I will carry and will deliver you.—I will be with thee.

I will instruct thee and teach thee in the way which thou shalt go. I will guide thee with mine eye.—I will never leave thee nor forsake thee.—Lo, I am with you alway, even unto the end of the world.

Be careful for nothing, but in everything by prayer and supplication, with thanksgiving, let your requests be made known to God. And the peace of God, which passeth all understanding, shall keep your hearts and minds through Christ Jesus.

MATTHEW 11:28; 2 CORINTHIANS 1:20; PSALM 91:15; ISAIAH 46:4; ISAIAH 43:2; PHILIPPIANS 4:6–7; PSALM 32:8; HEBREWS 13:5; MATTHEW 28:20; REVELATION 1:17

Five

In Affliction

I, even I, am he that comforteth you.   Isaiah 51:12

Another Comforter, . . . even the Spirit of truth.

He hath sent me to bind up the brokenhearted.–A man of sorrows, and acquainted with grief.

The eternal God is thy refuge, and underneath are the everlasting arms.–As one whom his mother comforteth, so will I comfort you.

For he doth not afflict willingly nor grieve the children of men.–What I do thou knowest not now; but thou shalt know hereafter.–Lo, these are parts of his ways: but how little a portion is heard of him!

The LORD is very pitiful and of tender mercy.—The Father of mercies and the God of all comfort, who comforteth us in all our tribulation, that we may be able to comfort them which are in any trouble by the comfort wherewith we ourselves are comforted of God.

JOHN 14:16–17; ISAIAH 61:1; ISAIAH 53:3; DEUTERONOMY 33:27; ISAIAH 66:13; LAMENTATIONS 3:33; JOHN 13:7; JOB 26:14; JAMES 5:11; 2 CORINTHIANS 1:3–4

Six

Thanksgiving Day

They shall not be ashamed that wait for me.

ISAIAH 49:23

Said I not unto thee that, if thou wouldest believe, thou shouldest see the glory of God?

O Daniel, servant of the living God, is thy God, whom thou servest continually, able to deliver thee? No manner of hurt was found upon him, because he believed in his God.

I prayed, and the LORD hath given me my petition which I asked of him.—My heart rejoiceth in the LORD.— Come and hear, all ye that fear God, and I will declare what he hath done for my soul. Blessed be God, which hath not turned away my prayer nor his mercy from me.

When the waves . . . arise thou stillest them. He maketh the storm a calm, so that the waves thereof are still; . . . so he bringeth them unto their desired haven. Oh, that men would praise the LORD for his goodness.— Blessed is the man that trusteth in him.

JOHN 11:40; DANIEL 6:20, 23; 1 SAMUEL 1:27; 1 SAMUEL 2:1; PSALM 66:16, 20; DANIEL 2:23; PSALM 89:9; PSALM 107:29–31; PSALM 34:8